Teaching Reading & Comprehension to English Learners, K–5

Margarita Calderón

Solution Tree | Press

a division of

Solution Tree

Copyright © 2011 by Solution Tree Press

555 North Morton Street
Bloomington, IN 47404

800.733.6786 (toll free) / 812.336.7700
FAX: 812.336.7790

email: info@solution-tree.com
solution-tree.com

Printed in the United States of America

15 14 13   3 4 5

Library of Congress Cataloging-in-Publication Data

Calderón, Margarita.

 Teaching reading and comprehension to English learners, K–5 / Margarita Calderón.

   p. cm.

 Includes bibliographical references.

 ISBN 978-1-935542-03-2 (perfect bound) -- ISBN 978-1-935542-04-9 (library edition)

 1. English language--Study and teaching (Elementary)--United States--Foreign speakers. 2. Second language acquisition--United States. 3. Multiculturalism--United States. I. Title.

 PE1128.A2C24 2011

 372.4--dc22

                 2011004292

Solution Tree
Jeffrey C. Jones, CEO & President

Solution Tree Press
President: Douglas M. Rife
Publisher: Robert D. Clouse
Vice President of Production: Gretchen Knapp
Managing Production Editor: Caroline Wise
Senior Production Editor: Lesley Bolton
Proofreader: Elisabeth Abrams
Text and Cover Designer: Jenn Taylor

ACKNOWLEDGMENTS

There are so many fantastic folks to thank for inspiring this publication!

Teachers and administrators from: New York City schools, in particular MS 319, PS 46, PS 279, and all new RIGOR and ExC-ELL schools; North Carolina State Department of Education Title III Office and the many ExC-ELL schools throughout the state; Region 1 Education Service Center in Texas and schools in the region; Kauai schools and central office; Granite School District ELL Office, Granite Park MS, and Granite schools; Yupi'it School District and schools; and Washington, DC schools.

My mentors and friends: Dr. Robert Slavin, director of the Center for Research and Reform in Education at Johns Hopkins University, who has guided and inspired my research; Andrés Henríquez, program officer of the Urban Education National Program at the Carnegie Corporation of New York, who believed in this project and funded it for five years; Rebecca Fitch and Tim D'Emilio of the U.S. Department of Education, whose advice and friendship have always encouraged my work with schools; my best friends and associates who have worked side by side with me in all our professional development efforts in schools, Liliana Minaya-Rowe, María Trejo, Argelia Carreón, Elma Noyola, Flo Decker, Jeanne Cantú, Ana Bishop, Lupita Espino, and Lili Trillo; and, of course, Robb Clouse, who kept insisting that I write this book.

Solution Tree Press would like to thank the following reviewers:

Timothy Boals
Executive Director
World-Class Instructional Design and Assessment Consortium
Madison, Wisconsin

Regina Boyd
English as a Second Language Program Specialist
Charlotte-Mecklenburg Schools
Charlotte, North Carolina

Argelia Carreón
Educational Consultant, Former Director of Bilingual Education and
Accelerated Learning
El Paso Independent School District
El Paso, Texas

TABLE OF CONTENTS

ABOUT THE AUTHOR

Margarita Calderón, PhD, is professor emerita and senior research scientist at the Johns Hopkins University School of Education. She has conducted research, training, and curriculum development for teaching language, reading comprehension, and content knowledge to K–12 English learners. Her work has focused on effective instructional processes, two-way and dual-language programs, teacher learning communities, and professional development for schools with language minority populations and striving adolescent readers. Dr. Calderón's research has been supported by the Carnegie Corporation of New York, U.S. Department of Education, U.S. Department of Labor, National Institutes of Health, and the Texas Education Agency.

A native of Juárez, Mexico, Dr. Calderón is a recognized expert in education with more than one hundred publications to her credit. She is a respected member of several panels and national committees, and she has been welcomed internationally as a visiting lecturer. Dr. Calderón has created and directed her own international institutes for administrators, teachers, and parents. She has experience as a classroom teacher, bilingual program director, professional development coordinator, professor of educational leadership graduate programs, and teacher supervisor.

Dr. Calderón earned a doctorate in educational management, applied linguistics, and organizational development through a joint PhD program at Claremont Graduate University and San Diego State University.

INTRODUCTION

Greater numbers of English learners (ELs) are enrolled in school every year. (The U.S. Department of Education officially calls these students limited English proficient [LEP] students. They are also sometimes referred to as language minority students [LMS]). Teachers and administrators are concerned with the large gap in reading and academic standing between ELs and students performing at grade level and want to know how to provide quality instruction to help close this gap.

My colleagues and I have completed several longitudinal studies in preschool to grade 12 and analyzed others while participating in national research panels. In doing so, we have accumulated a collection of school-based and instructional features that are working for all students. These features have been integrated and empirically tested in a professional development model called Expediting Comprehension for English Language Learners (ExC-ELL) through funding from the Carnegie Corporation of New York. We have since offered ExC-ELL professional development programs and on-site follow-up activities in various schools, school districts, regional educational centers, state departments of education, and universities for teams of teachers, coaches, and administrators. With this book, we are now bringing this information to you. Each chapter emphasizes the features that have had the greatest impact on EL success.

The instruction and professional development model that is described in this book has been promoted by many teachers and principals who faithfully implemented the model and saw great results even in their first year. The caveat is that those results were attained only by those schools that did not skimp on the time it takes to model, practice, and coach all components; the time teachers need to integrate it all into their lesson plans; and the time teachers need to meet in their teacher learning communities. The greater the time allocated to teacher development, the greater the results in student achievement (Calderón et al., 2009).

Traditional forms of professional development—a workshop here and there—are not set up to promote reflection on practice, collaboration, and active learning by everyone in the school (Darling-Hammond & Richardson, 2009; Elmore, 2002). When schools, districts, and departments of education address the topic of EL curriculum and instruction, they typically do so by offering only generic workshops on second-language teaching to ESL and bilingual teachers. Sometimes the workshops are offered to sheltered-instruction teachers or teachers who are interested in receiving credits or certification. These workshops are not designed to meet the needs of all teachers and administrators in a school or to build learning communities that address student needs with a systematic, comprehensive approach. Therefore, year after year, some schools maintain their status quo, while others embrace every possible solution and assign to teachers every quick fix that comes along. Some schools stay with what worked at one time, while others look for what works with some of their students. After capturing EL-focused professional development features through our longitudinal studies, we began to create the framework of this book.

It is important to recognize and assess social, emotional, and behavioral development within a language minority framework. This book addresses the language, literacy, and content instructional needs of ELs and frames quality instruction within effective schooling structures and the implementation of response to intervention (RTI). The framework has been empirically tested as a whole-school implementation approach and has been found to help schools attain faster and more effective results for all students, not just for ELs.

The common denominator is the integration of language, literacy, and content. The combination of these three components addresses the following weaknesses:

- The ESL/bilingual staff know a language, but they need to know more about teaching reading comprehension or content academic vocabulary. Bilingual teachers need to be fully biliterate (proficient in speaking, reading, and writing in both languages).

- General education teachers know which key vocabulary is important to teach in each subject area, but they do not know the syntactic structures or problematic words that nest those key content words and create difficulties for ELs.

- Reading specialists and special education teachers need to know more strategies to accelerate learning for ELs and other students.

- All teachers need to be familiar with new developments in EL pedagogy, technology, and assessment.

New instructional strategies and assessment processes energize and motivate everyone—especially the students. Dedicated educators who want to generate passion, commitment, and energy in meeting the challenge of quality instruction in every classroom can use this book to create momentum.

Whether you are beginning a small or whole-school learning community, the important thing to remember is that it must eventually become a whole-school endeavor to generate EL success. Success for ELs is contingent on the success of all teachers, administrators, and other school personnel who encounter ELs throughout the school year, and success for educators is built on effective professional development strategies.

This book promotes a whole-school approach, regardless of the number of ELs in the school or their language backgrounds. Because the majority of dual-language programs are Spanish-speaking, we have used Spanish throughout the book to represent the primary language, knowing that many large school districts have dual-language programs in five or more languages. Regardless of program variation, what matters most are the quality, fidelity, and sensitivity of instructional delivery.

Though ELs are quite diverse, there are some very basic categories of ELs that might help teachers identify their differentiated needs. There is also a wide range of services and programs that have evolved over the years; some are more beneficial than others. In chapter 1, we take a look at the categories of ELs and the benefits and drawbacks of nine different programs meant to address their needs.

Chapter 2 defines RTI in relation to ELs. Elements of RTI, such as diagnosing difficulties, selecting performance assessments, measuring learning on various dimensions, and preventing failure or falling through gaps, can be beneficial in ensuring quality instruction for ELs.

By the time students enter first grade, their vocabulary banks should consist of at least five thousand words in their primary language. Some ELs are well on their way to knowing this many words in English; others aren't even close. Chapter 3 helps educators build a strong foundation for literacy with quality interventions in preschool and kindergarten. This chapter was written by a guest author, Dr. María Trejo, who has managed early childhood programs in California for many years and is now working nationally to help design quality dual-language preschool and early childhood programs.

Whether or not students learn to read and comprehend grade-level texts by the end of first grade is the best predictor of student success in the twelfth grade (National Institute for Literacy, 2009; National Reading Panel, 2000). Chapter 4 offers strategies to ensure that ELs do not find themselves in academic jeopardy. This chapter was coauthored with Trejo.

Chapter 5 explores a systematic way of identifying choice words for ELs and other struggling readers to facilitate reading comprehension. These words are then carried through a lesson and meshed with related words to build larger vocabulary banks. Chapter 6 continues the conversation by offering explicit vocabulary instruction techniques for ELs. Teaching vocabulary using the steps and strategies offered also helps other reluctant readers.

Chapter 7 informs educators of the processes for developing language and literacy and offers strategies for creating a balanced instructional approach for teaching reading to ELs and general education students simultaneously.

Several models are widely—and effectively—used for teaching writing. Chapter 8 highlights popular strategies and adapts them for use with ELs.

Chapter 9 focuses on anchoring and assessing knowledge. Various unobtrusive strategies are offered for tracking the learning progression of individual students.

Chapter 10 explores the use of cooperative learning to motivate and engage students. Cooperative learning activities can also help students accelerate their language, literacy, and knowledge base while learning social skills. Dr. Liliana Minaya-Rowe, a co-designer and trainer for various EL programs, is the guest author for this chapter.

The sequence of chapters 5 to 10 mirrors the instructional and lesson development sequence for teachers: vocabulary, reading, writing, anchoring of content knowledge, and assessment. An effective teacher begins by parsing a text—chunking it into smaller units, eliminating the fluff, and identifying the big ideas and targets for learning. Next, he or she selects vocabulary to preteach before reading, to highlight during reading, and to teach after reading. Following vocabulary instruction is the reading strand, during which the teacher models a reading decoding or comprehension skill or strategy students are to use. The teacher assigns an activity that consolidates knowledge, language, and reading comprehension to make sure the students are learning. Reading establishes patterns that can be mastered through a writing segment to bring it all together. Finally, underneath productive learning and exciting instruction lie classroom management and cooperative learning for ample student interaction and mastery of new language, academic, social, and self-monitoring skills.

CHAPTER ONE

The Diversity of Students and Programs

A teacher who has ELs in his or her classroom has triple the work. He or she is teaching not only core subjects but also basic language and literacy—and often without the time and resources to put together effective lessons that fit his or her teaching style and the students' diverse learning needs. It is no wonder that such teachers feel unprepared. A first step toward helping teachers feel and be successful is identifying the different levels of language, literacy, and core knowledge of the students. Once those levels are identified, the appropriate type of instructional program or intervention can be designed.

EL Categories

The heterogeneity of ELs in the classroom can be overwhelming for a teacher. The following are broad categories of ELs and the characteristics of each:

- **Non-English speakers entering preschool or kindergarten.** Non-English-speaking children entering school for the first time may or may not have large vocabulary banks in their primary language, which makes a significant difference on how quickly they learn English. Some may have attended preschool where instruction was mainly in Spanish or another primary language. Others may have participated in an English immersion program with or without language support. Some may have attended a preschool where instruction was equally delivered in the primary language and English. Exposure to books, talk stories, and life experiences has a positive impact on such children's early learning.

- **Long-term ELs.** These students have been in English-speaking schools since preschool or kindergarten, are in fourth through twelfth grades, and still have not passed the required exams to meet the exit criteria for the "limited English proficient" classification. Some are second- or third-generation U.S. or Canadian citizens; immigrant newcomers are only 10–15 percent of the EL population in most schools (August, Goldenberg, & Rueda, 2010). About 85–90 percent of all ELs in middle and high schools are long-term ELs. Analyzing the number of their long-term ELs before sending them to middle school is part of elementary schools' success indicators. Middle schools need to request these figures from their feeder elementaries.

- **Newcomers or refugees**. Many newcomers or refugees are well educated. They are often highly literate and good at math, science, geography, and history. However, they need the word labels, the language, to communicate their knowledge. In some cases, these students do very well in math and other core courses but lag behind in language arts and reading. Such students need accelerated programs that focus on oral language development.

- **Students with interrupted formal education (SIFE)**. Some newcomers or refugee children have overcome huge obstacles to get here. Some may have missed two or more years of school in their native countries or not even attended school at all. Such students will need intensive immediate interventions in language and literacy before they can tackle grade-level subject matter.

- **Special education ELs**. Some students are identified as having special educational needs while the problem is actually an English language need. Some are underserved; the problem has been identified as a language issue when these students really have a learning disability. It is important to provide appropriate interventions and monitor students carefully to see if they are receiving the correct intervention.

- **Migrant/transient ELs**. Migrant families move among states throughout the year. Others move among schools in the same district. Some spend part of the school year in their native countries but return to the same school or a school in the same neighborhood. In such instances, education becomes inconsistent. Schools and school districts are required to keep records of the individual progress of migrant students and to address their states of learning as they come and go.

- **Exited or reclassified ELs**. In some cases, ELs are reclassified early, perhaps at the end of first or second grade, based on a faulty assessment. As these students move up the grade levels, their limitations become more evident. Schools are required to monitor students' progress for at least two years after they are exited from a bilingual program or are reclassified. Intensive interventions may be necessary during the first few months.

Consider these categories. Does your class or school have ELs with any of these characteristics? If so, which category has the largest representation?

Demand and support for programs addressing this diversity, along with the needs of general education, gifted, and special education students, are on the rise. Due to demographic trends indicating that schools are acquiring larger numbers of ELs (National Clearinghouse for English Language Acquisition, 2008), it is no longer acceptable to have a little program here and a pull-out or push-in intervention there for many of these students. As the No Child Left Behind Act (NCLB) is reshaped and federal policies look toward research-based instruction that embraces diversity rather than pigeonholes it, schools are likely to have better opportunities to encompass a more holistic approach to education that reaches more children.

English Language Proficiency Standards

The World-Class Instructional Design and Assessment Consortium (WIDA, www .wida.us) has been researching and developing assessments for ELs and extensively field-testing its products for many years. As of this writing, twenty-two states have joined the WIDA Consortium and use its assessments. WIDA's student identification assessment identifies six levels of language proficiency and development (as shown in table 1.1, pages 10–11). These levels can be used to quickly determine language proficiency and core content knowledge.

As part of the WIDA assessment system, consortium members developed the WIDA English Language Proficiency (ELP) Standards, which served as the basis for the Teachers of English to Speakers of Other Languages (TESOL) 2006 PreK–12 English Language Proficiency Standards. The ELP Standards are intended to aid in the design of curriculum, instruction, and assessment for ELs. WIDA has also developed the ACCESS placement test for ELs, which is based on these standards. The WIDA Consortium is an excellent source for tools that help assess and differentiate ELs' needs.

Programs for ELs

The regrettable reality that about 85 to 90 percent of ELs in middle and high schools are long-term ELs leads everyone to question what has been happening—or not happening—in the elementary schools. Are the current programs ineffective?

Table 1.1: Levels of Language Proficiency

Level of proficiency	Learners will process, understand, produce, or use:
6—Reaching	• Specialized or technical language reflective of the content areas at grade level • A variety of sentence lengths of varying linguistic complexity in extended oral or written discourse as required by the specified grade level • Oral or written communication in English comparable to English-proficient peers
5—Bridging	• Specialized or technical language of the content areas • A variety of sentence lengths of varying linguistic complexity in extended oral or written discourse, including stories, essays, or reports • Oral or written language approaching comparability to that of English-proficient peers when presented with grade-level material
4—Expanding	• Specific and some technical language of the content areas • A variety of sentence lengths of varying linguistic complexity in oral discourse or multiple, related sentences or paragraphs • Oral or written language with minimal phonological, syntactic, or semantic errors that do not impede the overall meaning of the communication when presented with oral or written connected discourse with sensory, graphic, or interactive support
3—Developing	• General and some specific language of the content areas • Expanded sentences in oral interaction or written paragraphs • Oral or written language with phonological, syntactic, or semantic errors that may impede the communication but retain much of its meaning when presented with oral or written, narrative or expository descriptions with sensory, graphic, or interactive support
2—Beginning	• General language related to the content areas • Phrases or short sentences • Oral or written language with phonological, syntactic, or semantic errors that often impede the meaning of the communication when presented with one- to multiple-step commands, directions, questions, or a series of statements with sensory, graphic, or interactive support

1—Entering	• Pictorial or graphic representation of the language of the content areas
	• Words, phrases, or chunks of language when presented with one-step commands or directions; wh-, choice, or yes/no questions; or statements with sensory, graphic, or interactive support
	• Oral language with phonological, syntactic, or semantic errors that often impede meaning when presented with basic oral commands, direct questions, or simple statements with sensory, graphic, or interactive support

Source: Adapted from Gottlieb, Cranley, & Cammilleri, 2007, p. RG-45.

Several types of programs for EL instruction exist. Most are only partial programs in which ELs are not integrated into the whole system. The few that take the whole-child and whole-school approach seem to be the most successful thus far (Calderón & Minaya-Rowe, 2011). Table 1.2 (pages 12–15) delineates some of the most prevalent programs. While the benefits and drawbacks are also included, it is important to remember that the implementation and continuous improvement of each approach are what matter. Please note that within this book, the term ESL is used to encompass all students who are learning English, even though it may be their third, fourth, or fifth language.

One problem with implementing an instructional program for ELs is that in some schools there may be only a small number of students with the same language background and as many as forty different language groups represented. In those cases, it is practically impossible to offer bilingual or dual-language programs. On the other hand, if the majority of the students are from the same language background, that provides a great opportunity to develop exemplary bilingual programs. Effective programs must be developed in response to the community of students in individual schools.

Regardless of the instructional program implemented, monitoring the progress of ELs is necessary. The following set of questions should be kept handy to act as a litmus test every six weeks:

- To what extent did ELs at each proficiency level progress these six weeks?

- On what standards (for example, oral, reading, writing, content) are they strong?

- What are their weaknesses?

Table 1.2: Programs for ELs

Type of Program	Key Features	Benefits	Drawbacks
Transitional bilingual education (TBE) programs	Students in kindergarten through third-grade classrooms receive instruction mainly in their primary language with thirty to forty-five minutes of instruction in ESL from kindergarten to third grade. After third grade, they transition to English instruction during the majority of the school day, until they are fully immersed in English by fifth grade. Early transition begins at second grade.	Students feel more comfortable and accepted in schools. Their primary language is developed to a basic literacy level before transitioning to English instruction.	Some programs keep the students in the primary language too long or do not develop academic English by third grade to help them catch up with their peers; consequently, they lag behind and become long-term ELs in secondary schools. In other cases, the primary language also erodes after third grade. High-quality TBEs can limit these drawbacks. The issue of when to transition to all-English instruction is always a major concern.
Maintenance programs/ dual-language (DL) programs	These programs offer instruction in both languages from kindergarten through fifth grade. In a few cases, the programs are also in middle and high schools. Most programs begin instruction in the minority language and add English each year until the third or fourth grade, when both languages are allotted 50 percent of the time. The 50–50 version of this program allocates equal time to each language from kindergarten through twelfth grade.	Programs enable students to develop both English and their primary language to higher levels of proficiency and literacy. The preoccupation with when to transition a student to English is not an issue with these programs. Students can benefit from continuous instruction in both languages.	Programs require extensive administrative support and quality instruction in both languages—two critical features that many programs still lack.

Two-way bilingual instruction (TBI) programs	These programs offer instruction in both languages from kindergarten through twelfth grade. Ideally, half the students are native speakers of English and the other half are native speakers of a minority language. Most programs begin instruction in the minority language and add English each year until the third or fourth grade, when both languages are allotted 50 percent of the time. The 50–50 version of this program allocates equal time to each language from kindergarten through twelfth grade.	All students become bilingual and biliterate, and learn how to respect and interact with a different culture. Students in 50–50 programs are able to pass tests in English and the minority language by third grade. The preoccupation with when to transition a student to English is not an issue with these programs. Students can benefit from continuous instruction in both languages.	Programs require more resources, quality instruction in two languages, extensive collegial planning, and administrative and community support. Some programs have had success with only majority students, while others have had success with only minority students, meaning that the instruction needs improvement.
Pull-out ESL/ bilingual programs	ESL instruction is typically offered in thirty- to forty-minute blocks in elementary schools or whole periods in secondary schools. Students are pulled out of their classrooms and grouped with one ESL teacher for basic oral English development.	ELs have one teacher they can relate to and who can address their language and schooling needs.	Some ESL/bilingual teachers have to work with multiple-grade-level students in the same group. When ELs are pulled out of class, they miss valuable content and peer interaction with English speakers. ELs fall behind in all subjects and may develop English language and literacy at a slow pace.

continued →

Type of Program	Key Features	Benefits	Drawbacks
Push-in ESL/ bilingual programs	An ESL teacher goes into a classroom to work with one or a few students, mainly translating or facilitating understanding during instruction by the general education teacher.	ELs are present for the content and language of the general education classroom. Such programs are potentially beneficial when there is one or a handful of ELs in a classroom.	As EL populations grow, it becomes impossible for teachers to push in and address so many students. ELs fall behind in all subjects and do not develop English language and literacy. Team teaching in this context becomes difficult for both teachers, unless time is allocated for daily planning.
Structured English immersion (SEI) programs	Implemented in elementary schools where teachers are highly skilled at teaching their general education curriculum with second-language strategies to help ELs learn content and English.	Beneficial for students and teachers when there are students from multiple language backgrounds within the class and bilingual instruction is not possible. If teachers are well prepared, ELs move smoothly into English and are able to keep up with core subjects.	Students' primary language erodes if not fomented at home. If the primary language is not accorded respect, recognition, or status, family communication suffers, as well as students' self-esteem and appreciation of their cultures.
English immersion (EI) programs	ELs are immersed in English-only classrooms in which teachers are not certified, credentialed, or prepared to teach ELs.	Very few students are able to benefit from such immersion in today's schools.	Students' primary language erodes. Students are rarely able to do well academically. There are too many obstacles for students and teachers.

Sheltered instruction (SI) programs	Programs are mainly implemented in secondary schools with teachers who are ESL credentialed and include some science, social studies, or math curricula into their sheltered English blocks. Elementary teachers who are certified also provide these programs.	In secondary schools, ELs learn English and some content concepts, usually in social studies. Elementary schools can structure similar programs.	Usually, there is not enough rigor. In secondary schools, the curriculum is often watered down and simplified to an extreme. ELs need several sheltered courses in order to master English literacy and core content. The same problem can occur in elementary schools, and ELs do not progress systematically in academic English and core subjects.
Whole-school programs	These are courses in secondary schools taught by general education teachers who have core subject credentials plus ESL certification or in-service training to teach language, literacy, and content in an integrated approach. At the elementary level, this approach is also used in dual-language programs, two-way bilingual programs, and effective structured English immersion or sheltered instruction programs.	ELs learn English vocabulary, reading comprehension skills, and writing skills for each content area. ELs are able to catch up and keep up with their native-English peers.	General education teachers need extensive in-service training and follow-up coaching to help them integrate language and literacy development strategies into their content lessons and instructional strategies. School administrators are reluctant to invest time and resources to help all teachers in the school receive this preparation.

- Which instructional strategies appear to be the most effective across all EL categories? For specific categories?

- Which instructional strategies need to be strengthened?

- Do the collective data substantiate the programs as configured? Do the programs need to be reconfigured?

A School's Commitment to Serving Every Student

The proper or improper identification and placement of students can make or break a school. Schools that get the attention of the Office for Civil Rights or schools that can't seem to get student scores to improve have usually neglected the identification and placement process. Some students get lost in the shuffle and are found too late. In some cases, students are not properly identified until years later or when they go to another school.

Proper identification is not complicated, but it does take time. To make the task easier, some schools select and train a team of five or more members, including teachers, an assistant principal or counselor, a parent, an ESL specialist, and/or a special educator. At the secondary school level, these are usually interdisciplinary teams with an administrator and special education and language specialists. This language assessment team sets up a system for reviewing assessments, placements, and ongoing progress of ELs. They keep individual records for each student, which include the student's primary language; scores for listening, speaking, reading, and writing in English and the primary language; any special education or gifted/talented programs; the credentials/certifications of their teachers; and test results from the required assessments. With this process, the proper identification and assessment of ELs is not on the shoulders of just one teacher; the whole school takes on the responsibility of serving every student.

Reflection Questions

The following questions are provided to initiate discussions on the topics and processes mentioned in this chapter.

For Teachers and Administrators

1. Develop a grid of the different types of ELs and the approximate number for each at every grade level.

2. What category has the largest representation? How can students be grouped? Develop another matrix for grouping students for specific interventions.

3. How will you assess the students to determine if they belong in those categories or to determine who needs an additional intervention? What assessments do you need to purchase or develop? What types of rubrics do you need to develop?

4. What types of instructional targets or interventions do you see needing a lot of attention? List the interventions (for example, vocabulary, decoding, social norms) and prioritize.

5. What is the best program or combination of programs for your students? (Think of the students, not the adults.) How can you build these into a whole-school approach?

For Universities, Districts, and Departments of Education

1. What are the best assessment instruments currently available to you?

2. How are you going to research and procure what is necessary for your teachers and student teachers, administrators, and leadership students to better diagnose ELs' knowledge, language, and literacy and their progress?

3. In what ways can you help current and future educators be prepared for the diversity of ELs?

4. What can you do to integrate ELs into a whole-school endeavor?

CHAPTER TWO

RTI and Quality Instruction

In the past, ELs who exhibited learning disabilities may have been underserved because school personnel did not have the knowledge and skills needed to identify and treat these students (Ortiz & Artiles, 2010). Now, RTI provides a great opportunity to address the needs of ELs in a whole-school effort. RTI involves providing services that ensure best practices in all instructional endeavors. Schools have options for providing such services but must address the three-tiered structure of increasingly intensive and focused instruction and interventions for students with academic or behavioral concerns.

RTI Explained

RTI stems from the Individuals with Disabilities Education Improvement Act of 2004. It is a three-tiered data-driven instructional system that provides access to quality instruction and intervention for all students. Once thought by educators to be exclusively for special education, many schools delayed implementing RTI across the board.

The National Center on Response to Intervention (www.rti4success.org) explains that the three-tiered system calls for benchmarks as follows: 80 to 90 percent of students must be achieving grade-level standards, but some may need additional support (Tier 1); 10 to 15 percent of students are one or two years below grade level (Tier 2); and 5 to 10 percent of students are two or more years below grade level (Tier 3).

Figure 2.1 (page 20) illustrates the tiers of RTI. Unless the teachers in Tier 1 provide quality instruction, many of their students, not just ELs, will fall through the instructional gaps into Tier 2. If the teachers who deliver Tier 2 interventions are not knowledgeable or specialized enough to quickly address those needs, their students will fall through the instructional gaps into Tier 3. If the teachers who deliver Tier 3 interventions are not well prepared to address students with special needs or those who are not proficient in English, those students will remain in Tier 3. The intent of RTI is to prevent students from getting into Tier 3 but, if they do, to move them quickly back into Tiers 2 and 1.

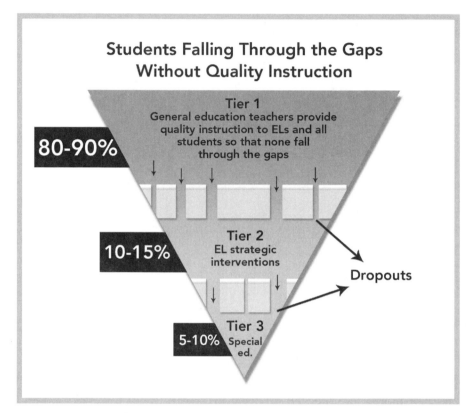

Figure 2.1: RTI triangle.

The core components of RTI outline a comprehensive instructional approach that includes screening, differentiating instruction, monitoring progress, and providing targeted interventions until the student shows measurable progress so as to require less and less support. The National Research Center on Learning Disabilities (2007) provides additional details about the key features of RTI. These are listed here with suggestions for their application to ELs:

- "School staff conduct universal screening of academics and behavior." If the required universal screening assessments have not been developed for ELs, assess students when possible in the primary language and in English in the four domains of listening, speaking, reading, and writing using the WIDA standards. When it is not possible to assess the primary language, use modified assessment procedures such as pointing, drawing, and taking more time. Assess knowledge of grade-level math and science concepts. Administer screening as quickly as possible at the beginning of the year and every six weeks thereafter.

- "General education instructors and staff assume an active role in students' assessment." Identify at-risk students with teacher input and interdisciplinary teams or language assessment teams. Consult parents. Enlist the services of professionals with appropriate qualifications or try other interventions before presuming a learning disability exists. For subsequent assessment benchmarks, hold data meetings to identify and understand more complex problems and to evaluate interventions. Interventions should enable students to move quickly from one proficiency level to another, at least every six weeks.

- "Standardized treatment protocol or an individualized, problem-solving model" is used. A problem-solving process can be used to identify the nature and degree of a problem. This process entails problem identification, problem analysis, goal setting, intervention planning, and outcome evaluation, and needs to include EL specialists. Observation protocols can also be used to identify problems and potential solutions when small teams of observers triangulate their observational data. Emotional, social, and behavioral rubrics can be used and sent home on a weekly basis.

- "Students receive high-quality instruction in their general education setting," and the "general education instruction is research based." While there are few research-based instructional programs that work for ELs as well as all other students, there is still a strong enough research base to choose from (Saunders & Goldenberg, 2010). For example, the National Literacy Panel has found evidence that cooperative learning and vocabulary and reading development can effectively form the basis of such programs (August & Shanahan, 2006, 2008). (Cooperative learning is also an effective classroom management tool that develops communicative, social, and collaborative skills.)

- "Continuous progress monitoring of student performance occurs" in identified areas of difficulty. Frequent assessments are used to measure the progress of language, literacy, content knowledge, and behavior. The frequency helps to prevent students from falling through the instructional gaps. These assessments or observation protocols should answer the questions: Which students need additional supports? Is the EL making progress, or is an instructional adjustment warranted? What are the specific areas (for example, phonemic awareness, decoding, vocabulary, reading comprehension, writing, or specific behaviors) that require better instruction, a specific intervention, or closer diagnostic examination?

- "School staff use progress-monitoring data to determine interventions' effectiveness and to make any modifications as needed." ELs in need of Tier 2 interventions will need additional instructional interventions in small groups during class time, as well as in after-school or Saturday academies. Students below the twenty-fifth percentile need at least ninety minutes a day of additional instruction to catch up as quickly as possible. The students who are in the lowest percentiles, or are most at risk, need to be assessed on a weekly basis in areas of concern and receive more time on interventions. Classroom observations are necessary to determine the quality of instruction. If a teacher is at risk of not providing appropriate instruction, that teacher should receive professional development right away. Differentiated professional development and coaching should be offered to address teachers' individual needs.

- There is a systematic assessment of "the fidelity or integrity with which instruction and interventions are implemented." Fidelity to a research-based model of instruction is critical. The three indicators of effective implementation—frequency, fidelity, and quality of implementation—correlate with student outcomes. Therefore, the observation protocols need to be frequent and systematic in order to determine if all three indicators are present in the classroom. Teachers also need appropriate materials and resources to carry out their tasks.

ELs benefit from having teachers who are highly interested in ensuring that their students make adequate progress in reading and who have the knowledge and skills to provide appropriate instruction. ELs will be better served if teachers and school personnel do not expect or accept low performance or view the ELs as undeserving of effective interventions (Francis, Rivera, Moughamian, & Lesaux, 2008).

Interventions in Dual-Language Programs

Schools with dual-language programs need to follow the same RTI guidelines. However, the following sections highlight some additional principles to consider.

Tier 1

Some ELs who enter English-speaking schools between grades 2 and 5 have adequate literacy knowledge and skills in their primary language, but their literacy skills in English are below average. These students have demonstrated the capacity to acquire reading skills and can now apply those skills to the acquisition of English literacy.

Tier 1 teachers should make sure that instruction in both languages is of high quality and adhere to the following guidelines (Vaughn, n.d.):

- Set high but reasonable expectations, and provide ongoing instructional support to ensure that these expectations are met.

- Do not wait for English oral language to meet grade-level expectations before providing reading instruction. For all English proficiency levels, begin teaching reading and writing from the time the students enter school.

- Promote language and vocabulary development throughout the day. Integrate academic language development into core instruction across subject areas.

- Provide opportunities for ample interaction through peer learning and small-group instruction.

Tier 2

Some students may have low literacy levels in both their primary language and English because they have not received adequate instruction in either language. These students require intensive literacy instruction or tutoring. Such interventions can be effectively implemented as early as first grade and throughout the elementary grades. Teachers who deliver Tier 2 interventions should adhere to the following guidelines (Vaughn, n.d.):

- Immediately provide intensive reading interventions to ELs who demonstrate low reading skills, but add vocabulary development to avoid interventions that become word reading without meaning.

- Ensure that interventions are sufficiently intensive in small groups (three to six students) for a minimum of thirty minutes each day.

- Explain and model behaviors for cooperative learning and social skills, and assist with emotional or identity issues.

- Maintain strong connections with parents.

Tier 3

After six weeks of Tier 2 interventions, there may be a small group of students who demonstrate low literacy skills in both their primary language and English even after receiving adequate instruction and interventions. These are the students most in need of testing for Tier 3 interventions.

ELs who are significantly behind in vocabulary and reading require intensive and extensive interventions that continue until the student is able to show adequate progress and benefits from vocabulary and reading instruction provided within the core curriculum. Teachers who deliver Tier 3 interventions should adhere to the following guidelines (Vaughn, n.d.):

- Provide a well-trained specialist—such as a bilingual education teacher, an ESL teacher with a strong background in literacy, or a learning disability teacher who has a strong background in and understanding of the educational needs of ELs—to implement the interventions.

- Make adjustments to instruction as necessary; the instruction may need to last for a significant period of time when students are making minimal progress.

- Consider other factors—such as family, personal attention, behavior problems, and classroom variables—that may need to be addressed along with the instructional interventions. A family-school team approach to problem solving may be very useful in interpreting factors that influence progress and designing instruction.

The instructional practices described in the following chapters can be implemented in all three tiers. Tier 1 teachers should consider implementing these instructional practices to prevent language and reading difficulties for all students, including ELs. Tier 2 teachers may consider implementing these strategies before or after school, at Saturday academies, or during special summer sessions for those ELs who need interventions in small groups or one on one. Tier 3 specialists working with ELs who have a more intense need of specialized services, ideally offered in the student's primary language, may also consider integrating the vocabulary, reading, and writing strategies into their interventions.

Attributes of Quality Instruction

There are certain attributes of quality instruction and implementation that have been identified by numerous researchers as being significant to the academic success of ELs. Johns Hopkins researchers found that ELs can do just as well in bilingual programs as in structured immersion programs by fourth grade, if certain programmatic features are in place (Slavin, Madden, Calderón, Chamberlain, & Hennessy, 2010). Other researchers have identified the same or similar features for elementary schools (Ortiz & Artiles, 2010; Lara-Alecio, Irby, & Tong, 2010) and middle and high schools (National Research Council, 2010). The National Literacy Panel on Language-Minority Children and Youth found basically the same features in their extensive review of the literature and confirmed the effectiveness of instruction in two languages when instruction is comprehensive and systematic (August & Shanahan, 2006, 2008; Slavin & Cheung, 2005; August, Goldenberg, & Rueda, 2010). These identified attributes of quality instruction and implementation are:

- **Comprehensive approach to teaching reading**. This includes phonemic awareness, decoding, vocabulary, reading comprehension, and writing for ELs in English or in English and another language for dual-language programs.

- **Special emphasis on vocabulary**. Schools espouse semantic awareness; vocabulary is taught throughout the day, with ample time for explicit instruction and student interaction in all subjects.

- **Equally exemplary instruction in English and the primary language**. High-level quality instruction is provided in all subjects in English and the primary language, particularly in dual-language / two-way bilingual programs.

- **Language and reading in the content areas**. Language, reading, and writing are taught for math, science, and social studies, not just language arts or ESL/ELD (English language development).

- **Same quality materials in both languages**. This refers to differentiated materials for tutoring students at different grade levels, family literacy materials, and take-home books.

- **Whole-school implementation of instruction**. All teachers and administrators, not just the ESL or bilingual teacher(s), become responsible for all ELs, because ELs are part of the school and eventually will be in other teachers' classrooms.

- **Professional development for all teachers, coaches, and administrators**. ESL and bilingual teachers are not the only ones who need to update their toolboxes. General education teachers, particularly for grades 3 through 6, who receive transitioned ELs or newcomers must be ready to teach with an approach of integrating language, reading comprehension, writing, and subject matter. Coaches and principals need to learn how to observe and give feedback when using new instruction techniques and materials. Principals need to know what to look for in EL classrooms.

- **Teacher learning communities (TLCs)**. TLCs are instituted and scheduled for at least thirty minutes per week, during which time teachers share strategies, analyze student progress, celebrate successes, solve problems, and motivate one another toward continuous learning.

- **Continuous coaching of teachers and monitoring of implementation**. The coaching and monitoring of quality implementation is part of measuring student progress. Students cannot advance if educators are not showing progress through systematic learning and the application of that new learning. Teacher learning correlates with student learning (Calderón, 2009).

- **Family literacy teams**. Families are offered materials to enhance vocabulary, reading, writing, and content at home. The school collaborates with parents on school attendance and provides services or social services referrals for children and families.

- **Assessments every six weeks at minimum**. Such assessments are used to gauge student progress, adjust instruction, and move students to more challenging levels or provide tutoring. When ELs with special educational needs are identified, they are placed in the appropriate programs quickly.

- **Tutoring for Tier 2 and Tier 3 interventions**. Intensive interventions in English and the primary language are provided by highly trained tutors or specialists when needed to ensure that no student lags behind grade level. Computer-based tutoring is available in addition to one-on-one tutoring. Assessments are used to determine when to stop tutoring or add a different focus.

- **Buy-in for more than one year's effort**. Educators realize that it takes more than a one-year effort to see significant results. By the second year, many schools begin to see exciting results; some even see dramatic results. It depends on the whole-school buy-in and the leadership commitment to the changes.

- **Excellent leadership**. The school's principal and assistant principals send positive messages and convey enthusiasm toward the sustainability of the attributes listed here.

- **Implementation visits by outside experts**. Outside experts conduct three or more implementation visits to observe each classroom, give teachers feedback, and set goals for improvement. They are also shadowed by the principal and coaches and model providing feedback on how teaching is reaching each EL, and assist in setting goals and next steps for each teacher. They submit reports after each visit.

- **Monthly and end-of-the-year reports on learning progressions**. Reports focus on teacher and student learning progressions and outcomes.

- **Monthly and end-of-the-year reports on school structures**. Administrative support, coaching effectiveness, family support, tutoring practices, attendance, and punctuality are analyzed in the context of student outcomes.

Prepare to Prevent Failure

English learners need explicit instruction on vocabulary, reading, and writing throughout the day—not just during ESL or the language arts block, but also during math, science, and social studies. As outlined by Race to the Top, RTI, and other education guidelines, students must show continuous progress in listening, speaking, reading, writing, math, science, and social studies. Therefore, it is to everyone's advantage to prepare a rigorous language, literacy, and subject matter program for ELs in kindergarten and systematically proceed with the same rigor through fifth grade. Of course, ELs will come into the school during different times of the year; thus, the school needs to be prepared with assessment processes and activities that allow students to show what they know and with Tier 2 and Tier 3 research-based interventions to help them quickly catch up to grade level if necessary.

The feedback loops generated by quick and frequent assessment activities help prevent student failure. They also demonstrate teacher success. Each time a teacher adjusts instruction and ELs show improvement, this is proof of learning progress and quality instruction.

Reflection Questions

The following questions are provided to initiate discussions on the topics and processes mentioned in this chapter.

For Teachers

1. What is the role of a Tier 1 teacher?

2. How do Tier 2 and Tier 3 teachers assist ELs currently? How can you intensify and better support their efforts?

3. What type of program has been selected for ensuring the success of ELs? Why was that program selected?

4. How can you and your colleagues make the program you select a whole-school effort?

For Administrators

1. How can you improve your school in order to improve learning for ELs?

2. Does your school improvement plan or success plan include the features listed in this chapter?

3. What are the tasks you need to undertake toward your school's improvement?

For Universities and Departments of Education

1. Are you supporting your schools in their efforts to address all students' needs? Can you provide assistance with reviews of the literature or presentations? Can you serve on their planning committees or language assessment teams?

2. How can you integrate the attributes listed in this chapter into teacher preparation programs?

3. How can you integrate these attributes into leadership development programs?

4. What resources are allocated to whole-school efforts focusing on ELs?

CHAPTER THREE

The Educational Needs of Young ELs

By María Trejo

Education reforms and interventions are needed for every grade. However, it is much easier to build a strong foundation with quality interventions in preschool and kindergarten, when students' needs are much more manageable and educators are teaching new skills, not remediating gaps.

Reforms have been targeted to address the "fourth-grade slump," the "wasted middle grades," the "desperate high school years," and, most recently, a "prekindergarten–kindergarten readiness gap." This early gap need not exist. It can be avoided with quality interventions that support early literacy development, the preparation and backing of more high-quality teachers, meaningful involvement of parents, and a consistent infusion of necessary resources. These practices are being articulated as part of prekindergarten–20 educational initiatives in many states. These initiatives are essentially major reforms of curriculum and student outcomes across the grades, preschool through college.

Young ELs need to be taught both foundational concepts and the classroom English necessary to succeed academically, and teachers need to have the necessary skill sets, resources, and tools to help these students acquire language and learn content. There are four distinct elements that educators must address when selecting materials, strategies, and interventions for young ELs:

1. The process of learning a second language

2. The importance of the primary language

3. Preliteracy in English

4. Family support

A teacher's understanding of how children acquire languages, when and how to maximize the use of the primary language spoken in the home, and how to model academic discourse in the first and second languages impacts how children learn language and important content (Tabors, 2008).

WHAT DOES THE RESEARCH SAY?

The early years are when educators can influence not only students' knowledge and skills but also their attitudes and aspirations (Chamberlin & Plucker, 2008).

Neglecting the early years or treating them as optional undermines the preK–20 educational structure (Takanishi & Kauerz, 2008).

ELs begin their early years of schooling with educational needs that the majority population does not manifest (Ballantyne, Sanderman, & McLaughlin, 2008).

Dual-language learners "are less likely than other children living in poverty to attend preschool, despite the fact that preschool attendance has more of a beneficial effect for Spanish-speaking dual-language learners than for any other comparable demographic group" (Ballantyne, Sanderman, & McLaughlin, 2008).

In the early years, literacy skills in two languages can develop at the same time (Society for Neuroscience, 2008), but there are unique skills and social norms associated with each language.

Selected states report that high-quality, comprehensive preschools can significantly boost the school readiness and later school achievement of children (Gormley, Phillips, & Gayer, 2008).

During the early years, children master foundational skills and concepts, develop attitudes towards school, and form ideas about themselves as learners (Shore, 2009).

The Process of Learning a Second Language

Knowing how a child develops a first language and acquires a second one helps teachers gauge what the student is ready to learn and what responses may be expected as he or she grows emotionally and acquires language(s). For example, second-language learners go through a period during which all they do is listen to the new language. This is often referred to as the "silent period" because they may not reproduce or speak the new language. Those educators who understand this stage know that they should not expect any oral responses from the learner during this period. The second stage of acquiring a new language is when the speaker copies or mimics the responses of others. These two stages may last a few weeks to many months; educators need to be patient and respect this time.

Many teachers have interpreted the first two stages of second-language acquisition as a waiting period during which the student cannot be forced to respond or speak the new language and either revert to teaching entirely in the primary language or to switching between the student's primary language and English because they believe that this will ensure understanding and be more comfortable for the student. However, in such cases, the consequences may be that the student's learning of the new language is delayed or not developed because:

- Teachers lower their expectations of the EL's learning abilities.

- Teachers reduce the rigor and richness of the curriculum.

- Teachers limit the use of rich academic vocabulary in both languages to shelter or protect the student.

- Teachers fail to check for understanding or learning progress.

- Teachers pass their low expectations, language-mixing practices, and limited use of English on to parents.

Educators are encouraged to learn how a child acquires a first and/or second language. Many educational agencies and departments of education publish guides in this field.

The Importance of the Primary Language

Educators often hear directives such as "Honor the primary language and use it— if resources are available" and "We don't have the time, money, or materials in every language, so teach in English." Overt efforts must be made to tailor the curriculum and strategies for ELs to facilitate second-language and literacy learning (Tabors, 2008).

It is not necessary for all teachers who work with ELs to be bilingual. What is important is the selection of the language of instruction, the designation of the adult who will be teaching in the primary language, the careful selection of materials, and the assigned roles of other support staff. There are basically three options for supporting the student's primary language and delivering instruction in the primary language:

1. In the first scenario, the classroom teacher is bilingual and biliterate. A teacher who is *bilingual* speaks both the language of the student and English. A teacher who is *biliterate* has had academic literacy training and reads and writes in both the primary language and English. This teacher can teach concepts in the primary language, as well as help the students learn English by keeping instruction in both languages separate during the day, without mixing languages, which is sometimes called code switching. Some students might code-switch, and that is fine, as long as they are progressing in the differentiation of both languages.

2. In the second scenario, the classroom teacher is monolingual English speaking but has the help of a biliterate instructional assistant who has the academic preparation in the primary language necessary to teach academic vocabulary and content. In this case, the teacher can plan with the assistant to ensure that the same concepts are taught in the primary language. The teacher in this scenario is the English-speaking role model.

3. In the third scenario, neither the teacher nor the assistant is biliterate. The teacher or assistant may be bilingual or have social language skills but not the academic vocabulary or professional preparation necessary to teach in the primary language. In this case, there are other strategies, such as: identify and invite community volunteers who are biliterate, ask the parents or older siblings to reinforce language and skills in the primary language at home, and seek the support of biliterate retired teachers or staff. However, the best solution is for these teachers to develop high language and literacy skills through intensive professional development.

It is critically important that students have the best language models possible in both the primary language and English and that the educators do not mix languages, or code-switch, during the delivery of their lessons. The classroom may be the only opportunity for ELs to listen to academic vocabulary and learn preliteracy skills in English.

Preliteracy in English

Preschool and kindergarten students need words and experiences to express their thoughts and to acquire new knowledge; they need oral language in both their primary language and English. Vocabulary and comprehension are intricately tied for these children. Their need to understand and be understood is much stronger than their need to learn the alphabet or the sounds of letters. Not understanding teachers and peers creates an anxiety in students that often hampers their ability and interest in learning or playing.

Children do not find it fun to sing rhymes and songs when they have absolutely no concept of why the sounds or jokes are funny. It is difficult, if not impossible, for a student to retain the concepts of syllable segmentation and deletion, onset and rime, phoneme segmentation and manipulation, rhyming, and alliteration activities when he or she does not know words like *cat*, *mat*, *mop*, and *mat*.

Given these considerations, the recommended sequence for teaching early literacy in two languages is the following: introduce and develop vocabulary, teach concepts about print, introduce alphabet recognition and word/print recognition, teach comprehension and age-appropriate text features, teach more difficult and abstract concepts, and teach writing.

First, introduce and develop vocabulary. ELs learn best from using nonfictional materials, manipulating concrete objects, and having hands-on experiences. A strategy that is popular with teachers when introducing new vocabulary or concepts is the total physical response (TPR) method, developed by James Asher, a professor of psychology at San José State University, in 1969 to aid learning a second language. Teachers and children act out the meaning of words through a simple game like Simon Says or a role-playing activity.

The five-step vocabulary strategy for young ELs follows:

1. Introduce the new word or phrase in a natural setting or with the use of concrete objects.

2. Explain the word using everyday language. Provide a child-friendly definition.

3. Give examples of the word in a variety of contexts. Use complete sentences.

4. Continue using the word at every opportunity.

5. Acknowledge the student's attempts at using the new word.

For example, during a unit on transportation and before visiting the train station, the airport, or the bus depot, the teacher introduces several words, such as *passenger*, *transportation, fare, station, board, baggage,* and *luggage,* by following the five-step process as outlined in table 3.1.

Table 3.1: Example of the Five-Step Process for Teaching Words

Introduce the new word or phrase in a natural setting or with the use of concrete objects.	Holding a piece of luggage, the teacher says, "We always need to tag our *luggage* before we go on a trip. The *luggage* is stored in the belly of the airplane." (Most likely, the teacher will also need to explain the word *belly.*)
Explain the word using everyday language. Provide a child-friendly definition.	The teacher explains, "The bags and personal things you take on a trip are your *luggage.*"
Give examples of the word in a variety of contexts. Use complete sentences.	In the pretend or play area, the teacher has the students pack small bags, write their name or draw a picture on a tag, and tie the tag to their *luggage.* The students show and tell others what is in their *luggage.* Students are asked to say, "I have . . . in my luggage. I am taking my luggage to . . ."
Continue using the word at every opportunity.	The teacher tells the students to ask their parents to show them what *luggage* they take on their trips, how many pieces of *luggage* they take on trips, and what happens if they lose their *luggage.* The next day, students are asked to share the answers to these questions. The teacher reads a story about a trip during which the characters take *luggage.*
Acknowledge the student's attempts at using the new word.	The teacher gives the student a sticker or teacher-made luggage tag to put on his or her suitcase every time the student uses the word *luggage.*

Second, teach concepts about print. Implicitly and explicitly expose students to print. Students will learn that people around them use print for many purposes and that print words carry meaning. For example, a teacher takes students to the zoo and immediately after the visit shows books and reads stories about zoo animals. The teacher explains the association between the lion that the students saw at the zoo, the word *lion,* and the picture in the book associated with the word *lion.* The teacher also explicitly explains to the students that printed words have meaning and that one can see and learn about many animals through books.

Third, introduce alphabet recognition and word/print recognition. As students become more confident with the oral language of the classroom, learn new words each day, and understand key concepts being taught, they will develop the foundation needed to learn that letters create words, that letters have a name, and that letters may have different sounds.

Fourth, teach comprehension and age-appropriate text features (for example, parts of a book, page numbers, turning the pages). Students will learn the difference between real and fictional events and that events have sequences. They will be able to construct simple narrative scripts because they will have built up a bank of words.

Fifth, teach more difficult and abstract concepts. After a teacher has completed steps one through four, phonological awareness, words and sentences, awareness of syllables, onset and rime, and rhyming can be introduced. ELs will be able to acquire and retain these abstract concepts because they will have had enough vocabulary and comprehension to appreciate what is being taught.

Sixth, teach writing. Help the students understand that signs can be used to represent ideas and concepts. They will begin to discern the differences between writing and other forms of communication like drawing.

This sequence for introducing preliteracy skills does not require a certain amount of time between the teachings of each skill. Rather, it emphasizes the need to develop understanding and vocabulary first, to ensure that the student will be predisposed, ready, and able to participate when he or she is being taught the more abstract and difficult language concepts and skills. For example, an instructional sequence could be designed as follows for bilingual or structured English immersion programs:

1. **First day**. The teacher selects a science or math book (nonfiction content), introduces and works with key vocabulary words and concepts, and discusses the content. The parents are asked to discuss the same key concepts and vocabulary in their preferred language that evening to make sure that the student fully understands.

2. **Second day**. The teacher rereads the text, reviews vocabulary, and asks the students to draw pictures of what they have read or to match key words to pictures. Using the same text, the teacher discusses concepts of print. Parents are asked to help the child find activities that are related to his or

her lessons or to take the child on a quick neighborhood field trip to expose him or her to the same topics.

3. **Third day**. The teacher involves the students in a classroom project such as building a zoo with cages, animals, towers, and ticket windows. Big class projects help students use new vocabulary, understand math and science concepts, develop schema of what they are learning, increase interest in learning, and make connections between oral language, print, and textbooks. Parents are asked to help construct parts of the zoo, to take the student to the zoo, or to show the student a TV program about animals in zoos.

4. **Fourth day**. The teacher introduces the letters that begin key vocabulary words previously taught or the names of animals, characters, or plants in the story being read. Parents are asked to explain what letters are, their names, and that each may have various sounds. It is best when parents can work on the same letters being taught by teachers. Children are capable of learning the alphabet and the concept of letter sounds for either language or both, as long as they have discrete language models for each.

5. **Fifth day**. The teacher introduces a phonological concept. If the students have limited vocabularies, listening to particular sounds and associating them with words just learned would be a first step. Over time, as the students become more confident and their vocabulary banks grow, awareness of words in sentences and the concept of sentences are introduced. Teaching awareness of syllables would be next, followed by onset and rime, and finally rhyming and alliteration.

This series is repeated throughout the year with every new big book or lesson. The time that it takes to cycle one series depends on the needs of the students, daily assessments of how the students are doing, pacing of lessons, and support from families and others. The emphasis is on explicit instruction of the five steps. Students can work at centers afterwards but mainly to reinforce what the teacher has taught. Explicit instruction must come first.

When introducing preliteracy and reading concepts to young ELs, teach subject matter at the same time. This can be done by carefully selecting nonfiction math, science, and social studies books and materials that incorporate preliteracy concepts and rich vocabulary.

ELs learn best when they are presented with big concepts in both languages, when ideas are fully developed, and when there is redundancy embedded in their materials. Teachers have more time to plan lessons, vary strategies, and enjoy the teaching process when they select large themes to teach and use the same texts to teach vocabulary, content, and skills. Materials and texts need to be carefully selected to ensure that they cover key concepts in the content areas, as well as provide opportunities to teach vocabulary and preliteracy skills. Neither the teacher nor the classroom materials should "overshelter" language and literacy. That is, the teacher and the materials should not use only basic vocabulary, simplify concepts, or superficially cover key concepts. Teachers need to stretch the learning of the students and trust in their ability to progress quickly.

The Nuview Preschool Center for Excellence uses an excellent strategy to help students learn literacy concepts and acquire languages: literacy trips. One such trip is to a local nursery. A bus full of parents and students, each carrying a clipboard, pencil, and paper, arrives. Their curriculum topic is "Caring for the World."

Parents and students spread throughout the nursery, exploring plants, soil, and insects, and interviewing staff. Parents lead the students, pointing out specific plants, parts of plants, colors, textures, and so on. The students are asked to call each element by its proper name and then draw a picture of what they see. The parents help the students write the name of the plant or element by the picture. Everyone has a wonderful day exploring and researching together. Literacy field trips produce excellent results for all students, and students take pride and pleasure in using new words that offer them more precise ways to refer to ideas.

Classes also include many effective oral language development and vocabulary activities. Staff and parents work together to select topics to explore or places to visit. Nonfiction books are used for read-alouds and dialogic reading. Comprehensive topics are selected. Staff adapt strategies such as "text talk" (Beck & McKeown, 2001) and the five-step process for teaching vocabulary (Calderón & Minaya-Rowe, 2011). When using text talk strategies, the teacher identifies two to four words in a text. The teacher reads each word again as it was used in the text, and the students are asked to repeat the word along with the teacher to create a phonological representation of the word. The teacher then provides a definition easily understood by the students and uses the word in a context other than that of the story to ensure full understanding. Teachers reinforce two to three new words daily by:

- Reading nonfiction books on the topic to students

- Exposing students to various child-friendly definitions of the new words

- Providing students with a variety of opportunities to use new vocabulary

- Incorporating literacy field trips (such as going to a hospital or grocery store) or large projects (such as building boats and testing them to see if they float)

Assessments of receptive vocabulary of students attending the Nuview Preschool Center for Excellence show four-point gains or greater on the Peabody Picture Vocabulary Test (PPVT). Oral language and concepts about print also improve. The results are impressive for several reasons. The majority of the students are ELs, but they are assessed—pre- and posttested—with the English PPVT. At Nuview, most ELs show greater growth than students who are native English speakers. Some students learn key words and concepts in Spanish, and some learn in English at school and in Spanish at home. Nuview staff believe that using nonfiction texts, providing students with carefully selected opportunities to practice new vocabulary, and teaching concepts through fun, concrete experiences such as the monthly literacy field trips are what make the difference in their students' learning and retention.

Family Support

Poor instruction affects all students, but more so those whose parents are not able to reinforce at home the foundations for academic success or teach their children in the language of instruction being used in schools (Raudenbush, 2009). Parents need to be encouraged to take an active part in their children's learning, to be told to help their children in the language they prefer or feel most comfortable with, and to understand the value of their participation in schools. Working closely with parents helps educators determine the level of assistance and support that can be expected from home and identify the most efficient language of instruction for the student, and it can help parents develop significant long-term changes within their families.

The critical time to reach a family is when the child is most vulnerable and impressionable, between birth and five years old. Families may differ in the number of members, level of formal education, preferred use of language in the home, values, goals, childrearing practices, immigration, migration, and acculturation backgrounds, as well as experiences with public agencies. Some parents may be surprised or confused when asked their opinions about the schooling they expect for their children. They may believe that such matters belong to the experts and teachers. Many parents feel intimidated because of their lack of knowledge of the school system or their limited English-speaking abilities (California Department of Education, 2009).

Successful early learning programs plan for a two-generation approach to include parents. Comprehensive family literacy programs incorporate center-based instruction, home visitations, adult literacy, parent education, and parent/child interactive literacy activities (Family Literacy Support Network, 2009). It is important that teachers recognize, respect, and rely on the potential of the adults in each family for expediting the learning of their children and for ensuring their readiness to transition through the various levels of schooling. A first and immediate step is to learn the beliefs and wishes of parents regarding the development of the primary language and the acquisition of English. Some parents may wish to develop, enhance, and maintain the language of the home for as long as possible. Others may wish to expose their children to social and academic English as quickly as possible. Whatever the wishes of the parents happen to be, it is important for teachers and staff to convey to parents that it is not necessary to make a choice between two languages. Children are capable of learning several languages simultaneously without being confused, delaying their learning, or sacrificing the primary language of the home. Staff can assist parents in making informed decisions by sharing research on how children learn multiple languages, information on the instructional resources to be used and the bilingual skills of staff available, and the educational goals of the center or school the child will be attending.

Students whose parents participate and assist with their education often have higher promotion rates, lower absenteeism rates, better grades, and higher school and community involvement, and are more likely to be performing at grade level and meeting grade-level standards. Children in preschools whose parents help them with their early literacy and social development are better prepared for kindergarten. They seem more confident, acquire larger vocabularies, learn more letters, are exposed to more concepts, and develop more social skills (Harvard Family Research Project, 2006; Epstein, 2005; Education Alliance, 1998).

What should educators ask of parents? The parents of students who are developing their primary language and learning English can be asked to focus on several specific areas:

- Ask parents to expand and reinforce oral language by rereading and discussing stories and books introduced by the teacher. Teach the parents strategies to do this. Most publishers now offer translations of main readers that can be used at home by parents. Parents should be encouraged to use their strongest language and conduct rich conversations with their children.

- Ask parents to expand and reinforce vocabulary by exposing their children to new experiences and carefully selecting words to use during the activities. Teach parents how to do this. Give them examples such as, "Such-and-such can be done when you take your children on nature walks around the neighborhood, during a visit to a museum, when exploring a grocery store, while visiting the doctor, or when you revisit vocabulary learned during the day at the school."

- Ask parents to expose their children to science and math concepts in whichever language they prefer. Make parents aware that their children understand and learn much more from nonfiction books and concrete experiences. Homes are full of objects and living things that can be used to engage children in important science and mathematical activities. The parent can point out the names and shapes of various objects in the home, on the playground, and in nearby buildings. While the child is learning the labels, the parent can write these down or help the child find the corresponding pictures and words in a geometry or shapes book.

- Ask parents to reinforce concepts when the child is playing. Parents know that children love to play and could play all day, but they are not always aware of the important concepts that children are learning during play. When parents become aware, they play more with their children and engage in activities that maximize the learning of new concepts and new vocabulary.

Educators often find parents to be much more effective partners when they are given opportunities and responsibilities. In one California family literacy program, parents have been asked to become "parent assistants" in the classroom as a way to give back to their centers. The parents are seen as people with gifts to share and needs to be filled. The program staff often comment about the wonderful results of the strategy for both adults and children:

> The "Parent Assistant" is learning multiple components when she assists in the classroom. She is learning about child development, practicing her parenting skills, and interacting with her child and with other children. And because she has to be on time, follow the instructions of the Lead Teacher, and is using her English language skills, is also engaged in the adult education component of family literacy. (Family Literacy Support Network, 2009, p. 6)

The U.S. Department of Education (www.ed.gov/pubs) has published booklets in

Spanish to help parents become involved in their children's education at home, including the following:

- *¡Imagínate!* (*Imagine!*) (Calderón et al., 2010a) contains activities to help children become good readers, develop their imagination and knowledge, retell stories, and begin emergent writing. It also gives parents a rationale for ensuring that their children become bilingual and biliterate.

- *Anhelos y Logros* (*Longings and Accomplishments*) (Calderón et al., 2010b) gives parents ideas on how to communicate effectively with their children and their children's teachers about teaching vocabulary and preliteracy skills. It lists the important concepts and literacy skills that preK to third-grade children should be acquiring and teachers teaching.

- *Palabras/Words* (Calderón et al., 2010c) focuses on teaching and learning academic vocabulary in the home. It provides multiple strategies and occasions for parents to introduce and use different types of words.

Reducing the Gaps

Educators and administrators have the opportunity to reduce emergent readiness gaps and persistent learning gaps in the public schools. Key to this intervention are:

- A thorough understanding of the learning process that ELs who are developing their primary language while learning a second language are experiencing

- The careful selection and preparation of biliterate teachers

- Conscious efforts to model and use appropriate academic language in either the primary language or English

- Avoiding the use of code switching, or mixing languages, for instruction

- Concerted efforts to assist parents so that they can be partners in the education of their children

- The rethinking and reordering of the teaching of literacy skills to children who come to school with limited vocabularies in any language

The type of training teachers bring to the classroom, the quality of their instruction, the content knowledge they master, and their capacity to engage pupils are all linked to significant differences in children's learning (Darling-Hammond, 2000;

Hill, Rowan, & Ball, 2005; Hamre, Pianta, Mashburn, & Downer, 2007). School factors are just as influential as home and family factors on student achievement, and the most important school resource in determining student achievement is teacher expertise (Darling-Hammond, 1997).

Reflection Questions

The following questions are provided to initiate discussions on the topics and processes mentioned in this chapter.

For Teachers

1. How can you add more vocabulary words to your daily teaching so that students' oral language expands?

2. How do you work with parents to reinforce vocabulary or to expose their children to more interesting vocabulary at home?

3. What science and math books do you have in your classroom that would be effective for teaching new vocabulary to ELs?

For Administrators

1. Do you need to organize workshops for teachers and parents to discuss how to support the students at home?

2. How do you identify, hire, and train biliterate teachers, instructional assistants, or volunteers?

For Universities and Departments of Education

1. Have you informed teachers about the importance of teaching oral language and vocabulary first in the preliteracy sequence? If not, how can you reinforce the message?

2. How can you work with publishers to develop children's materials that incorporate more systematic strategies for teaching vocabulary and comprehension?

CHAPTER FOUR

The Most Critical Year: First Grade

By María Trejo and Margarita Calderón

If a first grader is not beginning to read; does not know the difference between letter sounds and letter names; has limited oral language and vocabulary; does not have a basic understanding of mathematics, science, and concepts such as distance, height, and weight; cannot count; and has limited academic vocabulary in science and mathematics, the first-grade teacher needs to intervene—and quickly. Chances are, there is an academic and language gap between this student and average-achieving first-grade students. His or her vocabulary is probably three thousand to five thousand words behind other students of similar age; his or her comprehension and learning strategies are most likely quite limited; and there is a high probability that his or her parents are not aware that the child is already in academic jeopardy.

Who is most at risk of academic jeopardy? Children who did not attend preschool; children who are English learners; children who may have special educational needs; children who come from homes where the adults have very low literacy backgrounds; children who come from homes where there are no opportunities to visit parks, go on vacations, or go to the library; and children who do not have books at home to read or family members who read to them often. These are children who depend totally on their daily school experiences and the abilities of their teachers to help them learn.

There is much interest nowadays in providing comprehensive preschool experiences for children to prepare them for kindergarten. And in kindergarten, teachers are pressured to prepare students for first grade. There are associations for preschool educators, for kindergarten educators, for elementary educators; however, educators rarely organize to represent the needs of first-grade students or their teachers. First grade is a "silent year."

Too often, educators and family members do not pay much attention to first graders who are falling behind. Most figure that these students still have plenty of time to improve, to catch up. Educators often rationalize this lack of progress as "developmental immaturity." The goal in most schools is to prepare students to read and "read to learn" by third grade; therefore, many teachers believe that first graders still have two more years to learn basic concepts and English.

What tools do first graders need to help them learn and protect them against failure? All students benefit from the use of concrete objects to learn new and complicated concepts, instructional practices that include lots of modeling and repetition, classroom management practices that are taught and enforced with clear rules and routines, and strong parental participation in the academic life of the school, not just for social support. ELs and students with special needs require the same core practices as general education students but with added time, as they are working three times as much—having to acquire everyday language, academic language to communicate new content in various subjects, and the new content in those subjects.

Knowledge of written and oral English language conventions is essential for listening and speaking; it is important that students have good instructional models for both. Significant to the development of good sentence structure is the ability to speak in complete and coherent sentences. To learn and improve grammar skills, students need to hear, speak, and write correct usages of singular and plural nouns, and identify and correctly use contractions such as *isn't, aren't, can't,* and *won't* and singular possessive pronouns such as *my/mine, his/her, hers,* and *yours.* In first grade, students learn to capitalize the first word of a sentence, names of people and places, and the pronoun *I.*

Reading Instruction

The difference between reading instruction for ELs and general students is that ELs need more time with explicit instruction. While other students are silently reading, the teacher can do some intensive small-group or one-on-one reading instruction with the ELs. Additionally, students benefit from direct instruction using the same readers.

Consider this scenario. A first-grade teacher modeled learning unfamiliar words in context by reading the first page of a trade book aloud for the class, rereading a sentence, and using a fix-it strategy. Then, she used the overhead to illustrate the comprehension strategy by tracing with a marker how she went back and forth while reading that long sentence. Afterwards, she instructed the students to go to the bins of their classroom library, select a book to read, and apply the strategy. The twenty-six students selected twenty-six different books to read. The teacher walked around the room trying to monitor each student, to help those who were barely attempting to decode word by word the first sentence of their book, and to keep everyone on task. The six ELs in the class were either thumbing the pages, pushing the book aside, or sitting quietly wondering what to do.

We have observed this often in classrooms. Some teachers argue that they can't preteach the vocabulary words when the students are going to read different books, they can't monitor independent reading because the students haven't learned to read independently, they can't help the ELs because those students need so much more help than the others, and they sense that some of their students are becoming discouraged with reading, others are only pretending to read, and some read fluently without comprehension. Arguments such as these are not helping ELs develop reading skills. On the contrary, they are helping ELs develop a bad taste for reading.

During effective explicit reading instruction, the teacher uses a book slightly above the students' reading level to model fluency and types of reading strategies students can use. However, the teacher needs to model the reading strategies again with the book the students are going to read. It should be the same book so that all students are literally on the same page. Of course, the teacher has already pretaught five or so key words from vocabulary tiers 1, 2, and 3 (see chapter 5). These words will help ELs and all other reluctant readers when they read and try the strategy that the teacher wants them to apply. The students read with a buddy so they can practice fluency, pronunciation/prosody, and new words, and make sense of what they are reading as they stop and talk about what they read every few sentences. As they engage in partner reading, they practice the new vocabulary words, forming sentences and clarifying meaning.

Teachers should assess ELs in first grade—or subsequent grades for students with interrupted formal education who are reading at a first-grade level—on a regular basis for progress in oral language and beginning reading skills. Some may need small-group instruction with lower than first-grade readers, more decoding, or more vocabulary.

ELs and Centers

It is important to offer a variety of opportunities for students to learn from the teacher, to work with peers, and to practice new skills, especially for struggling students and those who are learning a second language. In addition to small-group and differentiated instruction, instructional centers provide these opportunities. Centers can be designed for specific content areas of instruction, to reinforce skills and to provide students with ample opportunities to express what they know and receive feedback from other students and the teacher. Centers can be set up for all students and be differentiated for ELs at the same time. For example:

- **Reader's Theater Center**. Books that contain lines for different readability levels can be used at these centers. Students can practice fluency and pronunciation, learn new words, build listening skills, learn to take turns, and perform in front of an audience.

- **Listening/Reading Center**. Listening/reading centers are especially useful when teaching speaking, listening, and oral vocabulary and comprehension. ELs need to hear sounds and words from native speakers of the language to develop an ear for new sounds and unique variations of a new language. These centers can provide such opportunities from either teachers or recorded materials.

- **Computer Center**. ELs and other students can practice phonemic awareness, pronunciation, vocabulary, math, science, sequencing, following directions, and technology skills on the computer.

- **Writing Center**. Students can practice everything from letter formation to completing sentences by writing lists, stories, summaries, and cooperative stories.

- **Experiment Center**. ELs benefit from hands-on experiments in science and math. Discovery develops critical thinking even if the language skills are limited. ELs can team up with an English speaker and conduct experiments or solve math problems, then do a collaborative summary of what they learned.

- **Conversation Center**. Students practice conversations with adults—teachers, teacher assistants, or parents/volunteers.

WHAT DOES THE RESEARCH SAY?

According to the research (National Governors Association Center for Best Practices & Council of Chief State School Officers, 2010; WIDA Consortium; California Department of Education, 1999, 2000, 2003, 2010), essential skills for first grade are found in seven instructional areas: word analysis, fluency, vocabulary development, reading comprehension, writing, the academic language of mathematics, and the academic language of science.

Instruction addressing *word analysis* should consider the following:

Instruction in phonemic awareness begins in preschool, continues in kindergarten, and concludes with more complex activities by the middle of first grade.

Good readers rely primarily on the letters in a word rather than context or pictures to identify familiar and unfamiliar words (Ehri, 1994). Students must be explicitly taught the blending of individual sounds into words to assist them with the word-recognition process.

Students progress from vowel-consonant and consonant-vowel word types to consonant blends, vowel digraphs, and letter-sound associations.

Instruction introduces inflected endings and word roots to extend the students' word-recognition abilities.

Instruction addressing *fluency* should consider the following:

Students read aloud fluently in a manner that resembles natural speech.

On average, first graders increase their reading fluency approximately 2.10 correct words per week. By the end of the academic year, students should be reading about 60 words per minute correctly (Fuchs & Fuchs, 1993).

Students must develop fluency so that they do not spend their energy decoding words instead of focusing on comprehension (Stanovich, 1994).

One technique often used to increase fluency is repeated readings of the same text to develop familiarity and automaticity (Samuels, 1979).

Most important, knowledge of words—lots of words—will increase ELs' fluency.

Instruction addressing *vocabulary development* should consider the following:

Students need to learn two types of vocabulary: basic words associated with grade-appropriate concepts (for example, animals, foods) and the words students hear and read in stories and informational texts that assist comprehension.

Vocabulary development requires explicit instruction in specific concepts or words and word clusters through multiple exposures to a broad range of words in stories and nonfiction texts (Calderón, 2007a).

First graders need explicit instruction on how to use context and surrounding text to understand the meaning of unknown words.

ELs may be learning language and concepts in two languages, with English labels only, or a combination. Learning both languages simultaneously accelerates word knowledge (Calderón, 2007b).

Instruction addressing *reading comprehension* should consider the following:

Students develop listening comprehension through teacher read-alouds and modeling of the use of how, who, what, when, and where questions to clarify information in the text or the meaning of words and sentences.

Students learn and expand their knowledge of vocabulary by retelling the central ideas of expository text or narrative passages.

Students learn to recognize various features of text and the common signals in texts that help with comprehension and writing.

Students learn concepts of print, text features, and text structures by previewing text with teachers.

Teachers preteach new vocabulary and review previously learned ideas and vocabulary relevant to the new text.

No matter how limited in English, students are invited to share previous knowledge and related experiences.

Teachers flag expectations for what the students will be learning and the learning routines and expected behaviors.

Instruction addressing *writing* should consider the following:

Instruction combines penmanship, spelling, documentation, and formation.

Spelling is taught explicitly in the context of reading and writing so that students become aware of letter-sound correspondence and the phonemic structure of words.

Teachers plan many opportunities for daily writing and to practice spelling new words, presenting only one spelling rule or generalization at a time.

Students learn to read words and to write those words, and to spell high-frequency words correctly.

Students improve penmanship, printing legibly and spacing letters, words, and sentences appropriately.

Students practice and progress through the stages of the writing process: prewriting, drafting, revising, and editing successive versions.

Students write brief expository descriptions of a real object, person, place, or event, using sensory details.

Instruction addressing the *academic language of mathematics* should consider the following:

Students understand the concept of ones and tens in the place value system and the terms *less than*, *equal to*, *greater than*, *smaller than*, *plus*, *minus*, *total*, and *how many*.

Students understand the concept of adding and subtracting small numbers, and they solve problems. They understand the terms *total*, *how many*, *how much*, *how long*, *left over*, and *at least*.

Students use simple measurement units, locate objects in space, and extend patterns using graphs, shapes, and sizes. They understand the terms *count*, *estimate*, *measure*, and *identify*.

Students can describe simple data and analyze them to solve simple word problems.

Instruction addressing the *academic language of science* should consider the following:

Students learn the properties of solids, liquids, and gases—freezing, melting, heating, dissolving, and evaporating.

Students write brief expository descriptions about people, places, things, and events by answering the questions of who, what, when, how, and where.

Students learn about the needs, functions, and names of animals and plants. They understand terms such as *sunlight*, *habitats*, *soil*, *living organisms*, *survive*, and *adaptations to survive*.

Students learn that properties of substances can change when they are cooled, mixed, or heated, and understand the terms *evaporate*, *condensation*, *expand*, and *melting*.

The Importance of Conversation

It has been documented that adults, both teachers and parents, spend just a few minutes daily speaking with children (Aldridge, 2005; Dickinson & Snow, 1995). Conversations are usually commands, such as "Don't forget your lunch," "Do your homework," and "Clean your room." The ways in which caregivers talk and read with children and the type of conversations they have affect the development of oral language skills that are the critical underpinning for students' reading and writing achievement. It is important that teachers and parents set aside time and plan for conversations with children. Conversations need to be engaging, real, learning opportunities for children to extend or practice vocabulary, and focused on developing targeted skills.

This is especially crucial for ELs. Interesting, relevant, and meaningful conversations with parents provide nonthreatening situations in which to speak in their primary language, English, or a combination of both. Teacher talk provides ELs with the opportunity to practice newly learned vocabulary, clarify new ideas, negotiate new meanings, and build rapport. Instructional conversations help the teacher assess whether or not the student understands the new skills being taught (Peregoy & Boyle, 2008; Calderón & Minaya-Rowe, 2011).

The following two scenarios illustrate the use of interesting topics for conversations and the inserting of real concepts to engage children. They also illustrate how parents, with a bit of forward planning with the teacher, can support the child by introducing or reinforcing concepts that coincide with the teacher's lessons.

Dialogue 1 provides children with an opportunity to use abstract language:

> A parent is making *mole*. While roasting a dried red pepper, the parent asks the child, "Why do you think that I am roasting the pepper? What is going to happen to the pepper if I roast it too much? What will happen if I peel it and then soak it?"
>
> That same week, the teacher is conducting a science experiment on things that shrink and expand with heat and water. The teacher asks the students, "What do you think is going to happen to the dried fruit if I submerge it in hot water? What will happen to the tomato if I put it in hot water?"

Dialogue 2 provides children with an opportunity to use language for mathematical reasoning and concrete problem solving:

> The parent says to the child, "You know that there are four children in our house, you and your three brothers. Each one of you uses a pair of socks, or two socks each. Close your eyes and see if you can tell me how many pairs of socks you all use at the same time." After the child responds, the parent asks, "How did you figure it out? Can you tell me how many individual, or single, socks you all use when you go to school?" After the response, the parent again asks the child to share how he or she arrived at the answer. The parent can choose more difficult activities as the child learns and progresses.

That same week, the teacher at school works on solving problems orally and teaches students to estimate answers and then to check their calculations. The teacher uses concrete items to illustrate and reinforce vocabulary concepts such as *add to, take away from, all together, half of them, about how many, subtract from, double,* and *twice as many.* The teacher says, "In my shoe box, I have two mangoes, three peaches, five kiwis, and two pears. About how many total pieces of fruit do you think I have? Do you think that I have more than ten or fewer than ten? Who wants to tell me how many actual, total pieces of fruit are in the shoe box?" The teacher asks the child who estimates or knows the actual number, "How did you figure it out?"

Parental Partnerships

It is at this grade level that parents often start withdrawing from active involvement in school activities and stop helping their children at home. Many parents of ELs no longer feel comfortable participating because they believe that their English proficiency level and academic preparation are insufficient to meet the needs of their children or negotiate the activities of the school. Continued involvement exposes them too much. Parents often report that first-grade schoolwork becomes too difficult for them to understand. In addition, parents of ELs have the same reasons for dropping their involvement as other parents: they do not feel welcome or useful; they work too many hours; or they lack transportation (Hoover-Dempsey & Sandler, 1997). However, students still need daily support and instruction from their parents—their first and most important teachers. Parents can introduce or reinforce concepts in either language, through multiple experiences, using a variety of concrete objects found at home, or by asking the older siblings to help the younger ones do activities or homework.

Many parents do not know how to best help their children. They do not know the sequence of lessons, key concepts to teach, standards to be learned, academic levels of students, how to diagnose learning difficulties, or the best textbooks and materials to use. Parents need the teacher to show them how to support the child and how to introduce or reinforce concepts. Most parents are very interested in learning how to work with their children.

Whole-school approaches to parent engagement provide a myriad of ways to empower parents to work with their children. Schools can schedule after-school or before-school classes for parents during which they are taught strategies for working with their children, including: how to prepare for field trips, how to study for a test, how to write simple sentences, how to conduct instructional conversations, how to use dictionaries, how to estimate the total cost of groceries while shopping, how to memorize information, how to keep journals, how to rewrite homework, how to distinguish the various book genres, and so on. The educator is not expecting the parent to become an instructor but to support what the classroom teacher is teaching and to reinforce the big concepts being covered in school.

Although first grade is critical, all other grades are important along the continuum of a student's education. Each year reinforces what the student has learned, adds to his or her knowledge base, and stretches his or her potential. No academic year should be taken for granted. The students should be assessed continuously so that both educators and parents are aware of how the child is progressing.

Reflection Questions

The following questions are provided to initiate discussions on the topics and processes mentioned in this chapter.

For Teachers

1. What steps can you take to communicate the importance of first grade to other teachers, administrators, and parents?

2. What resources can you secure to review the skills and knowledge that first-grade students bring to the classroom, that they need to develop, and that may cause the most difficulties?

3. What information should you communicate to parents to ensure that they assist you with the education of their first graders?

4. How do you select the best assessments for your students? What does research say about translators and about translating tests versus developing and norming tests for EL populations?

5. How do you intervene with students who are already showing signs of falling behind when they enter first grade?

For Administrators

1. How do you ensure that your first graders have the same resources and attention as the students in other grades?

2. How do you support team building and planning among your kindergarten, first-grade, and second-grade teachers?

3. What additional resources, personnel, or professional development opportunities do your first-grade teachers need?

4. Have you analyzed and used the data available to determine how well students in your first grades do? Have you assessed the data to determine who are ELs and who may have special learning needs?

5. How do you increase parental engagement and support to assist the students with their daily school activities?

6. What have you done to assess the progress of first-grade ELs in your school?

For Universities and Departments of Education

1. What do your state or provincial data say about how well first-grade students do, how ELs do in first grade, and how students with special needs do?

2. What special training has been designed, what materials have been developed, and what assessments have been reviewed or created to enhance the knowledge base and skills of first-grade teachers?

3. What type of preservice or professional development should you offer to first-grade teachers with ELs?

CHAPTER FIVE

Selecting Words to Teach

Verbal ability has long been the basis of grade-level tests, college entrance exams, and graduate-level selection tests, and vocabulary knowledge is one of the best indicators of verbal ability (Graves, 1986; Stenberg, 1987). Due to the low literacy levels of students in grades 6 through 12, there has been a renewed interest in teaching vocabulary from preschool to twelfth grade. Chapter 6 will detail the process of teaching vocabulary, but before an educator can teach vocabulary, he or she must select which words to teach.

Academic Language

In selecting words to teach to ELs, one must have a thorough understanding of "academic language." The term *academic language* has been defined by various practitioners since Jim Cummins first wrote about it in 1979. Some simply differentiate it from "conversational English" or "schoolyard English." Researchers William Saunders and Claude Goldenberg (2010) define academic language as "the specialized vocabulary, grammar, discourse/textual, and functional skills associated with academic instruction and mastery of academic material and tasks" (p. 58). Jeff Zwiers (2008), who works with teachers and schools on the development of language, literacy, and content, explains academic language as "a set of words, grammar, and organizational strategies used to describe complex ideas, higher-order thinking processes, and abstract concepts" (p. 20).

In essence, *academic language*—or *academic vocabulary*, as it is sometimes called— is the language of schooling and careers. It is a particular way of using words and conveying status, knowledge, and persona (Calderón, 2009). In elementary schools, academic language is built from kindergarten up to fifth grade so that students are ready to be successful in middle school.

Fifth-grade academic vocabulary is not just content words such as *species*, *democracy*, and *equation*, or words that appear on tests such as *effect*, *allow*, *therefore*, *criteria*, and *distinct*; it is also the little words, such as *in*, *on*, *at*, and *so that*, and the multiple meanings of words such as *body* or *power*. For ELs, academic vocabulary begins the moment they step into the classroom. It's all academic for them—when to use *in*, *on*, and *at*; when to write *cell* or *sell*; and the difference between *some* and *sum* when they hear it in the teacher's rapid explanation.

Academic language, or academic vocabulary, consists of:

- All the words that are presented during phonemic awareness activities

- All the words that students are exposed to when being taught basic phonics

- Words associated with concepts in core subjects, as well as all the words in the sentences that nest those concepts

- Formal syntax and grammar that nest those concepts and words

- Words and phrases used for understanding, explaining, discussing, reading, and writing concepts in math, science, social studies, and language arts texts and tests

If ELs do not know these words, it will be very difficult for them to participate fully in any lesson or gain sufficient understanding to learn any subject.

Strategic Selection of Words

There is a wide range of language levels in each classroom due to age and grade-level spans, linguistic and cultural differences, learning disabilities, or differences in educational experiences. Since educators cannot teach every word in the science, math, social studies, or language arts texts that the students need to read every day, they must be selective and strategic and choose the words that are the most useful in learning the content and concepts and those that students will need to use to describe, question, or summarize what they have learned—not to mention those on their tests.

Educators can use the following steps to select words to teach for any passage and any subject. Selected words come not only from textbooks but also from any text used in the course of the lesson, such as that from websites and trade books. Words to teach also include commonly used phrases and directions that a teacher uses and that beginning ELs need to learn in order to participate in all activities.

Step 1: Parse the Text

Peruse the text you will be using, whether for science, social studies, math, or language arts. If it contains too many words that might be unfamiliar, divide, or "chunk," it into smaller, more manageable units. Next, underline the words your students absolutely must know to understand and learn this content. If it's a short story, poem, or chapter of a novel, select the words that are most important to the story (for example, those concerning plot, setting, and characterization).

Step 2: Address Standards

Think about the words that address language, literacy, and content standards. The WIDA guidelines recommend answering the following question: what is the language ELs need to process or produce to describe, explain, compare, evaluate, identify, sequence, classify or categorize, predict, question, or match (Gottlieb, Cranley, & Cammilleri, 2007)? The verbs in the standards ("Students will *describe*...") explain the writing and reading processes students will need to master. Therefore, the words in the standards are themselves important vocabulary words, but they also imply a host of other words. For example, table 5.1 lists the functions, strategies, and skills that are usually found in language arts or reading standards. Students are expected to develop these skills to meet the standards. But, in order to be proficient at describing a sequence, for example, ELs need language such as *first, second, next, additionally, concurrently,* and *finally.*

Table 5.1: Examples of Language Functions, Reading Comprehension Strategies, and Writing Skills

describing	defining	enumerating
classifying	comparing/contrasting	making inferences/hypotheses
summarizing	identifying	interpreting
explaining	organizing	retelling
predicting	asking and answering questions	making connections
visualizing	monitoring comprehension	determining important information
sequencing	finding the problem's solution	finding cause and effect

Step 3: Categorize the Words

Categorize the words that you have underlined into three tiers as described in the next section, selecting no more than five or six for each tier. If you have considerably more than that, the text may be too difficult for your students. It will

WHAT DOES THE RESEARCH SAY?

Command of a large vocabulary frequently sets high-achieving students apart from less successful students (Graves, 2006).

The number of words heard in an hour by children of poverty is about 615; by middle-class children, about 1,251; and by children of professionals, about 2,153 (Hart & Risley, 1995).

The average six-year-old has a vocabulary of approximately eight thousand words (Sénéchal & Cornell, 1993).

Active participation by students during teacher read-alouds contributes to vocabulary growth. For example, open-ended questions, function-attribute questions (as opposed to pointing without speaking), and multiple exposures to words during shared reading facilitate students' production of those words (Robbins & Ehri, 1994; Cunningham, 2005).

Vocabulary in kindergarten and first grade is a significant predictor of reading comprehension in the middle and secondary grades (Cunningham, 2005; Cunningham & Stanovich, 1997) or reading difficulties (Chall & Dale, 1995).

Effective instruction encompasses: teaching individual words; extensive exposure to rich language, both oral and written; and building generative word knowledge (Nagy, 2005).

ELs benefit from discussions about cognates, affixes, pronunciation, decoding, multiple meanings, phrasal clusters, and idioms using the word in question (Calderón et al., 2009).

take too long to teach all those words, and the comprehension will be stunted at best. If there are several more words that your ELs might need, that is an indicator that they may need a special intervention from an ESL teacher who can preteach those words. If you don't have enough words, the text is too easy or doesn't have enough conceptual substance.

Three Tiers of Vocabulary

Words can be categorized into three tiers as suggested by Isabel Beck and her colleagues (Beck, McKeown, & Kucan, 2002). (Please note that these tiers are specific to vocabulary and are different from the RTI tiers.) Teachers categorize words in three tiers for the purpose of modeling ways to approach unfamiliar words and to develop depth and breadth of word knowledge. Posting lists of tier 1, 2, and 3 words helps students develop semantic awareness and knowledge of how to analyze and categorize unfamiliar words themselves.

Tier 3

It is easiest to begin selecting words for tier 3. These are words that are subject-specific. Grade-level trade books and textbooks often highlight in bold the tier 3 words as the most important words and include them in a glossary. These words tell us immediately what discipline is being studied, as shown in table 5.2.

Table 5.2: Sample Tier 3 Words

Math	Science	Social Studies	Language Arts
rectangle	germ	government	personification
denominator	atom	bylaws	shifty character
balanced equation	osmosis	congressional districts	cause and effect
pi	matter	capital	inference
nth power	power surge	power of attorney	powerful potion
divide	cell division	divide and conquer	divisive

About 40 percent of tier 3 words are cognates with Latin-derived languages, such as Spanish, French, and Italian. Cognates are words that sound, are spelled, and have meanings that are similar across languages. Table 5.3 provides examples of cognates. Teachers can use cognates to aid comprehension and spelling. For example, students will recognize and remember patterns in suffixes in words such as *correction* and *corrección*. This metalinguistic analysis helps students zoom in on spelling patterns and better understand English.

Table 5.3: Cognates

English	Spanish
rectangle	rectángulo
govern	gobernar
personification	personificación
denominator	denominador
osmosis	ósmosis
radical	radical

Unfortunately, there are also false cognates. These words sound, are spelled, and look similar across languages, but they have different meanings. Table 5.4 provides examples of false cognates. In the last two rows, the French and English words are cognates, but the Spanish and English words are false cognates.

Table 5.4: False Cognates

English	Sounds like	But is in Spanish	. . . in French
library	librería (bookstore)	biblioteca	bibliothèque
story	historia (history)	cuento	histoire/conte
exit	éxito (success)	salida	sortie
success	suceso (event)	éxito	succès
character	carácter (personality)	personaje	caractère

Tier 2

Tier 2 words may be the most ignored when it comes to vocabulary instruction. The tier 2 category includes phrasal clusters, idioms, polysemous (multiple meaning) words, information-processing words, connectors, sophisticated words, and words to provide specificity to describe a concept (see table 5.5 for examples). These are the words that nest the tier 3 words. They hold together the meaning of a complex word.

Table 5.5: Sample Tier 2 Words

Phrasal clusters	stored energy, skim through, run your hand over, stimulus package, over the course of
Idioms, social function words/clusters	In your dreams. Break a leg. It's over his head. You can lead a horse to water, but . . . I'm just looking. I'm good. I know what you mean [agreement]. If . . . then . . . The problem is solved by . . .
Polysemous words	trunk, power, cell, left, right, light, prime
Information-processing words	apparent, assortment, assumption, basis, crucial, display, illustrate, generate, effect, affect, allow
Connectors	subsequently, although, as well as, however, as a result of, in order to, in contrast, for instance
Sophisticated words and words to provide specificity	shuddered, scrutiny, celestial, wholesome

Tier 1

These are simple words known by virtually all general education students within an age group, but not necessarily by ELs. ELs may not have the background knowledge for the concept, may not recognize the spelling or the pronunciation, or may not recognize the cognate or false cognate (see table 5.6 for examples). Although tier 1 words are the easiest words in a text, they are the hardest to identify for instruction because teachers may not be able to guess ahead of time which ones ELs know or need.

Begin by selecting those you think they will need. Then, as you observe and listen to the ELs conduct their partner reading and discussions on what they read, you will be able to identify other words they need.

Table 5.6: Sample Tier 1 Words

Spelling	tough, phrase, highlight, toothache
Pronunciation	sell/cell, axis/exes, ship/chip
Background knowledge	skyscraper, lawnmower, blender, parka
False cognate	embarrassed, exit, success, character

An Example

Using the following passage, a teacher selected tier 1, 2, and 3 words:

> The Role of the Sun
>
> Without our closest star—the sun—Earth would be a dark and chilly place. Although it is 150 million kilometers (about 93 million miles) away, the sun plays a huge role in Earth's climate. Energy from the sun heats Earth's atmosphere and surface. The sun keeps the plane warm and hospitable to life. (Benchmark Education Company, 2010, p. 9)

To get a more accurate sense of which words to select, she asked one of her ELs in level 3 (on a scale of 1 to 5 in terms of English proficiency), who was fairly fluent in English but lacked comprehension skills, to do a read-aloud/think-aloud of the paragraph. As the student read each sentence in the passage, he was to report what he understood from that sentence. This gave the teacher insight as to which words should be assigned to tier 2, since they were absolutely necessary to the meaning of the tier 3 words in the sentences where they were found. The reading also revealed which simple words needed to be clarified and should therefore be classified as tier 1.

With the help of her student's think-aloud, the teacher was able to select and categorize words as shown in table 5.7.

Table 5.7: The Teacher's Selection of Words for Posting and Teaching

Tier 1 Simple words	Tier 2 Process, idioms, phrasal clusters, sophisticated words or terms	Tier 3 Story-specific words, key vocabulary
without	although	climate
chilly	plays a huge role	atmosphere
away	hospitable	energy

The teacher also knew some Spanish and checked with the EL student to confirm which words were cognates with Spanish—*climate, atmosphere,* and *energy.* However, she also noted that there were false cognates in that passage—*chilly* and *hospitable.* The student thought *chilly* was *chile* (the hot spice) and that *hospitable* was *hospital.*

The teacher posted the tier 1, 2, and 3 words on chart paper to use during preteaching of vocabulary and kept them there for quick reviews and as words to use during writing activities until the next lesson. During the preteaching segment, she highlighted the cognates and false cognates for her other Spanish-speaking students and emphasized pronunciation for words she noticed were difficult for the EL student who read the passage aloud: *without, chilly,* and *away.* At first, the other students were surprised that she was quick-teaching (using drawings, gestures, or pictures) easy words and highlighting cognates (since not all were Spanish speakers), but they soon began to appreciate learning some Spanish and getting clarity on even the simple words they thought they knew.

Your Turn to Try It!

In figure 5.1, select vocabulary for tiers 1, 2, and 3 from the lesson, and fill in the vocabulary tiers chart.

Lesson Topic: A Change in Climate

Grade Level: 4–5

Content Objective: Interdependence of living things, climate, and the environment

Reading Comprehension Objective: Identify cause-and-effect examples

Language Objective: Learn tier 1, 2, and 3 vocabulary

WIDA Standard: Identify cause and effect from oral discourse and from text

A Change in Climate

By Emily Sohn

From one day to the next, weather can have a big effect on your life. When it rains, you have to stay indoors or carry an umbrella. When it's cold, you have to bundle up.

Over the course of hundreds, thousands, and millions of years, weather trends affect life on Earth in more dramatic ways. Ice ages or long droughts, for example, can wipe out certain types of plants and animals. Although many species manage to survive such extreme, long-term climate shifts, their living conditions also change. (Sohn, 2004)

Vocabulary Tiers Chart

Type of Words	Tier 1	Tier 2	Tier 3
Polysemous words			
Phrases, clusters, bundled-up words, idioms			
Cognates			
Connectors, transition words			
Homophones			
Others			

Figure 5.1: Exercise for selecting vocabulary words to teach.

There is no one way to categorize words, and there is often a fine line between categories for some words. Groups of students are different, and they will have different needs every year. Nevertheless, it is important to find a systematic approach to identifying the vocabulary words to teach that fits your style and meets the needs of all your students.

Quick Tips for Selecting Words to Teach

These quick tips offer some important reminders about selecting vocabulary words:

- When teachers work with grade-level colleagues or in vertical teams to identify vocabulary words to teach, they create a powerful collection of key words that are aligned across subjects and grade levels. Thus, more powerful student results are obtained. This type of collegial work creates a climate of semantic awareness for both educators and students in a school.

- When trying to determine the vocabulary to teach, select the words that are most important for:

    + Formal discourse between teacher and student and student and student regarding standards or goals

    + Comprehending the text the students are about to read or listen to

    + Use in students' formal writing

    + Success on tests

    + Future academic and economic status

- Also, ask yourself these questions: What are the tier 1 and 2 words that are tied to understanding the tier 3 words? From that list, which words are most important? Which words do you want the students to use?

Reflection Questions

The following questions are provided to initiate discussions on the topics and processes mentioned in this chapter.

For Teachers

1. Why do you need to sort vocabulary into three categories?

2. Why should you select words from each subject you teach?

3. In what ways can you organize your planning time to address this approach?

For Administrators

1. How will you make it easier for teachers to create the time to select vocabulary?

2. What type of professional development activity can you plan to provide for this focus on vocabulary?

For Universities and Departments of Education

1. What do you need to do to help your teachers be more aware of the semantic and vocabulary needs of their EL students?

2. What criteria will you set to select textbooks that are more appropriate for this task?

CHAPTER SIX

Teaching Vocabulary

Vocabulary words give beginning ELs the tools to accelerate their learning and begin to feel comfortable contributing in class. Vocabulary needs to be an integral part of teaching and learning. However, the quality of vocabulary instruction is very important. Memorizing isolated lists of words and copying definitions and sentences from the board do not produce vocabulary growth. Drawing pictures of a word does not necessarily lead to a student using the word. Attempting to understand the word through its context doesn't always help ELs because there may be several other words in that context that they do not understand.

Knowing a word means a student:

- Knows its meaning when reading it in a variety of texts

- Can pronounce and spell the word correctly

- Recognizes characteristics of the word, such as multiple meanings

- Can explain its meaning within the context of reading

- Can use it as a natural part of his or her writing repertoire

To effectively teach vocabulary, educators must provide explicit instruction, which entails: presenting both student-friendly and formal definitions; offering multiple exposures to a word in multiple forms; ensuring understanding of meaning(s); providing examples of a word's use in phrases, idioms, and usual contexts; highlighting characteristics or word parts; ensuring proper pronunciation and spelling; and, when possible, teaching a word's cognate or false cognate in the student's primary language. Whether gifted or just learning English as a second language, students need explicit and varied instruction to build solid word power.

Teaching vocabulary should be pervasive throughout the school. The more teachers are involved in systematic vocabulary instruction, the faster ELs, disadvantaged students, and special education students learn and succeed. Evidence of this accelerated learning is found in school MS 319.

In 2006, MS 319 was one of the lowest performing middle schools in New York City. In 2008, the school was recognized as the "Best Middle School in New York City"! If you walk through the halls, you will see tubes seemingly emerging from the floors with newspaper clippings, text downloaded from the Internet, and sticky notes with comments from students sharing their opinions about current events and today's economy. One hall is filled with science themes, bulletins with student writings about scientific processes, and vines hanging from the ceiling with long prepositional phrases, idioms, and information-processing words that about 40 percent of the student population is still learning. In a prealgebra classroom, an ESL teacher preteaches vocabulary before the math teacher presents a lesson. Another ESL teacher is in the back, recording teacher-student interactions in order to give feedback to the teachers during their lunch period. The math students in this class are 90 percent ELs. At the end of the period, they take a test on the SMART Board, using their clickers.

Teachers like to tell their visitors that extensive explicit vocabulary instruction became the basis of EL success and their school making adequate yearly progress (AYP). They argue that without understanding 80 to 90 percent of the words in a sentence, in a paragraph, or in a test question, a student cannot possibly grasp the concepts to be learned or respond to a question, much less enjoy math, science, social studies, and literature. They lament the fact that out of the 60 percent of ELs in the school, 46 percent were long-term ELs when they came to the school. They had been in English-speaking elementary schools since kindergarten! Some were fairly fluent speakers of English, but their literacy skills had been hampered by the lack of vocabulary instruction in their elementary grades.

There were also many native English speakers in the classrooms who were struggling readers because their word knowledge was limited. Thus, integrating rich vocabulary and reading into math, science, and social studies helped all students perform better on tests and feel better prepared for high school.

Levels of Word Knowledge

Word knowledge exists on a continuum ranging from absolutely no knowledge of the word to rich and powerful knowledge of the word (Graves, 2006). In classrooms with ELs, this entire range is likely represented, and small-group instruction on vocabulary will be helpful to the students on both ends of the continuum.

WHAT DOES THE RESEARCH SAY?

Effective vocabulary instruction has to start early, in preschool, and continue throughout the school years (Nagy, 2005).

Teaching vocabulary helps develop phonological awareness (Nagy, 2005) and reading comprehension (Beck, Perfetti, & McKeown, 1982).

Robust instruction offers "rich information about words and their uses, provides frequent and varied opportunities for students to think about and use words, and enhances students' language comprehension and production" (Beck et al., 2002, p. 2).

Vocabulary instruction needs to be explicitly taught before, during, and after reading to help ELs catch up with the words they are missing (Calderón et al., 2005; Calderón & Minaya-Rowe, 2003).

Vocabulary instruction needs to be long-term and comprehensive (Nagy, 2005) for ELs (Carlo, August, & Snow, 2005; Calderón et al., 2005).

There are four components for teaching vocabulary: "(1) providing rich and varied language experiences; (2) teaching individual words; (3) teaching word-learning strategies; and (4) fostering word consciousness" (Graves, 2006, p. 5).

Active participation by students during teacher read-alouds contributes to vocabulary growth. For example, open-ended questions and multiple exposures to words during shared reading facilitate students' production of those words (Robbins & Ehri, 1994; Cunningham, 2005).

Isabel Beck and colleagues (2002) identify the following different levels of word knowledge:

- **Level 1—No knowledge of the word**. The word *fastidious* is not likely known by most third graders.

- **Level 2—General sense of the word**. ELs who have heard *fastidioso* might know that it has a negative connotation, judging from their parents' tone.

- **Level 3—Narrow, context-bound knowledge**. In the sentence "He chooses his words with fastidious care," *fastidious* means "very attentive to and concerned about accuracy," which is very different from the archaic meaning of *fastidious* from Latin and dropped in late Middle English, which was "disagreeable" or "distasteful."

- **Level 4—Forgetting the word**. At this level, students know the word but are not able to recall it readily enough to apply it in a meaningful way.

- **Level 5—Depth of word knowledge**. This refers to a rich, decontextualized knowledge of a word's meaning(s) and its relationship to other words or other language(s)—for example, knowing that *fastidious* has a certain meaning in Spanish and another in English. It also means that ELs understand how a word is used in idioms.

Some students will be at level 1 with most words; others will fluctuate between levels depending on the complexity or novelty of the word. Students who are at level 1 with more than 50 percent of the words in a text will need an intensive intervention outside of class or more small-group or one-on-one instruction. Students who are at level 5 should be given opportunities to do more wordsmithing. In bilingual or dual-language classrooms, avoid translation for level 3–5 students. They need to grow accustomed to thinking, listening, speaking, reading, and writing in English.

Many of the instructional approaches used to teach vocabulary to general education students (Graves, 2006; Beck et al., 2002; Nagy, 2005) and the research on second-language vocabulary development (Grabe, 2009; Stahl & Nagy, 2006; Hiebert & Kamil, 2005; Carlo et. al, 2005; Calderón et al., 2005) were tested in classrooms with large and small groups of ELs (Calderón & Minaya-Rowe, 2003; Calderón, 2007a, 2007b, 2009). Based on those findings, some of the premises and approaches were adapted or changed to guide teachers' delivery and lesson designs for the ExC-ELL project. The explicit instruction of vocabulary developed for ELs became a three-part vocabulary approach: (1) preteaching vocabulary before reading or an instructional event, (2) teaching vocabulary during reading and discussions, and (3) teaching vocabulary after reading and during anchoring of knowledge.

Preteaching Vocabulary

Preteaching vocabulary is the most important instructional step in any lesson, yet it rarely happens! Many teachers introduce a word by asking the students, "Who knows what this word means?" After a barrage of wrong or partially correct guesses, the students are left wondering which meaning was right. Some teachers write the word and its meaning on the board for the students to copy. The word and definition are copied, but no learning takes place. Other teachers send their students to the dictionary, and the students copy the shortest definition, which is probably the wrong definition for the context.

Explicit preteaching of vocabulary is the best way to avoid confusion and ambiguity and to help students truly understand a word. A seven-step process for introducing words can be used at the beginning of a lesson, before a teacher read-aloud, or before students are to read a text. The tier 1–3 words can be taught as a whole-class or small-group process.

Seven-Step Process

The seven-step process lends itself best to teaching tier 2 and 3 words because those are more sophisticated and complex. The preteaching steps should provide the opportunity for oral production and exposure to the written word in context. The steps should move quickly so that no more than two or three minutes per word or ten to fifteen minutes for all the words are spent in preteaching key vocabulary. Teachers should leave plenty of time to model reading strategies and for students to read, verbally summarize, and write.

Following is the seven-step process:

1. The teacher says and shows the word, and asks students to repeat the word three times. This helps pronunciation and introduces the print version.

2. The teacher reads and shows the word in a sentence (context) from the text. This helps the students remember the word in context when they begin to read.

3. The teacher gives the dictionary or glossary definition(s). This provides exposure to formal English and what the students will encounter later when they are proficient enough in English to use a dictionary.

4. The teacher explains the meaning with student-friendly definitions or gives an example that students can relate to. The teacher uses simple language, familiar examples, pictures, props, movement, or gestures to help students comprehend the meaning or multiple meanings.

5. The teacher highlights an aspect of the word that might create difficulty: spelling, multiple meanings, false cognates, prefixes, suffixes, base word, synonyms, antonyms, homophones, grammatical variations, and so forth. Students will do more in-depth word study on what was highlighted later on.

6. The teacher engages all of the students in an activity to orally use or own the word and concept—for example, a think-pair-share activity. *Writing the word, drawing, or other word activities should come later, after reading.* First, students need to use the word orally in a variety of ways. ELs need to produce the word ten to twelve times orally during the preteaching segment.

7. The teacher assigns peer reading with oral and written summarization activities and explains how the new words need to be used or how students will be accountable for these words.

It is important that the students see the steps written out. The teacher can use chart paper, the blackboard, a PowerPoint presentation, or a whiteboard to present the seven steps. (For kindergarteners, seeing the words under each tier will suffice.) See table 6.1 for an example of how to present the seven steps.

Table 6.1: Presentation of the Seven Steps

The teacher says and shows the word, and asks students to repeat the word three times.	Say "manage" three times.
The teacher reads and shows the word in a sentence (context) from the text.	Although many species manage to survive such extreme . . .
The teacher gives the dictionary or glossary definition(s).	(1) succeed in doing something difficult; (2) to be in charge of, to run: *manage a company.*
The teacher explains the meaning with student-friendly definitions or gives an example that students can relate to.	I managed to lose ten pounds by exercising.
The teacher highlights an aspect of the word that might create difficulty.	*Manage* is a polysemous word. *Manejar* is the cognate.
The teacher engages all of the students in an activity to orally use or own the word and concept.	Think-pair-share: What have you *managed* well recently?
The teacher assigns peer reading with oral and written summarization activities and explains how the new words need to be used or how students will be accountable for these words.	Remember to use *manage* in your summaries.

Teaching Tier 1 Words

Most tier 1 words will be concrete words that can be demonstrated easily through visuals, motions, and gestures. Whiteboards facilitate quick drawings and photos from the Internet. The WIDA Consortium (Gottlieb et al., 2007, p. RG-21) provides strategies for teaching tier 1 words quickly and efficiently. They list examples for sensory supports such as real-life objects, pictures, and physical activities;

for graphic supports such as charts, graphs, timelines, and number lines; and for interactive supports such as partners, triads, cooperative group structures, and the Internet. As long as the ELs are orally producing the word in meaningful activities and contexts, any of these will work.

Explicit Instruction for Tier 2 Words

Tier 2 includes more complex words and longer phrases. The seven-step process is still used, but an emphasis is placed on words and phrases as described in the following sections.

Teaching Polysemous Words

Polysemous words, words that have multiple meanings, can be introduced with two or three meanings, but always emphasize the meaning that is used in the text the students are about to read. Most students will be familiar with the multiple meanings of words like *trunk*, but not necessarily the ELs. In such cases, ask the students who know a meaning to role-play it and have the class say the word three times.

Teaching Long Phrases

Idioms, noun phrases, and prepositional phrases need to be taught as whole chunks. For example, *on the spur of the moment, break a leg, from one day to the next,* and *as well as* are easier to learn when the whole term is presented and practiced.

Teaching Connectors and Transition Words

Why do students speak in simple sentences? Why do their writings look the same all the time—same simple words, disconnected paragraphs, and same transition words, such as *because, and, then,* and *next*? Connectors and transition words not only help oral expression but also help students write cohesively (see table 6.2, page 74).

Teachers can post these connectors and transition words on charts or distribute them as laminated handouts for students to keep in their desks for continuous use. Some teachers glue them on folder tents placed at the center of the tables during student discussions. Others hang them with yarn from the ceiling directly at the students' eye level. Then, during discussions, teachers ask students to use different words when posing or answering questions or expressing any of the function or skill objectives for that lesson.

Table 6.2: Connectors and Transition Words

Function	Sample sentence starters, connectors, and transition words
To describe cause and effect	because, due to, as a result, since, for this reason, therefore, in order to, so that, thus
To compare and/or contrast	and, also, as well as, in addition, likewise, moreover, by the way, or, but, although, however, in contrast, whereas, nevertheless, on the other hand, while, on the contrary, by comparison, ironically, yet, even though, just as
To give examples	for example, for instance, in particular, such as, in this situation, to illustrate, to demonstrate, in fact, indeed, in this case
To describe a sequence	first . . . second . . . , subsequently, following this, next, finally, concurrently, additionally, meanwhile
To bring to conclusion or describe results	in conclusion, ultimately, as a result, finally, thus, therefore, hence, accordingly, as we have seen, as we have shown, this led to, in essence
To conduct polite discussions	apparently, probably, likely, might, rarely, seldom, at times, sometimes, occasionally, theoretically, on the one hand, on the other hand

Teaching Specificity and Sophisticated Words

Tier 3 words are not the only sophisticated or difficult words; many tier 2 words are just as complex. For example, *accuracy, additive, crucial, depict,* and *deplete* are tier 2 words that are found on formal exams. If ELs are to do well on those tests, it behooves us to teach those rich words, along with more refined adjectives and adverbs. Long-term ELs use the same simple words over and over because *they have been allowed to get by with such small vocabularies!* That is why they do not move from one level of English proficiency to another quickly enough. Employing strategies to increase their vocabularies and adding words that provide more specific descriptions are the best interventions for moving ELs from one level to another.

Teaching Cognates and False Cognates

As mentioned previously, cognates are words in different languages that look alike and have the same meanings. When pointed out, cognates help bilingual students comprehend many content-specific words. It is better to see the word in writing because the pronunciation often varies considerably and may be difficult to understand.

Cognates also help bilingual students become better spellers. Spelling differences between cognates have patterns that help ELs predict and remember the correct form in English (for examples, see table 6.3). These features need to be explicitly taught by bilingual teachers.

Table 6.3: Suffix Patterns Among Cognates

Nouns	Adjectives	Verbs	Adverbs
-ion = -ión	-ous = -oso	-ate = -ar	-ly = -mente
action/acción	curious/curioso	decorate/decorar	absolutely/absolutamente

Word roots and affixes can also be learned much more quickly by bilingual students or students with Spanish-speaking backgrounds because of cognates (see table 6.4).

Table 6.4: Affixes Among Cognates

	Nouns	Adjectives	Verbs	Adverbs
English	alphabet	alphabetic	alphabetize	alphabetically
Spanish	alfabeto	alfabético	alfabetizar	alfabéticamente
English	favor	favorable	favor	favorably
Spanish	favor	favorable	favorecer	favorablemente

It is important to also point out false cognates—those words that look similar but have different meanings. For example, *library* is not *librería*; it is *biblioteca*. *Character* means disposition or moral values as well as personality, which is the same for *carácter*, but *personaje* is the character in a story or play. Thus, some words are both cognates and false cognates. I call these "polysemous cognates." Other examples include: *consentir*, which means to consent but also to spoil or pamper people; *masa*, which means *mass* (indefinite matter or group of people) but also dough for bread or for tortillas; *Mass* (religious ceremony) is *misa* in Spanish. Dictionaries of cognates and false cognates can help sort out all of this.

Teaching Vocabulary During Reading

Since you don't want to spend more than ten to fifteen minutes preteaching vocabulary, some words will have to be taught while reading. For example, the teacher reads a paragraph aloud and models for the students how to stop and think about the word and its context. The following sections highlight several other ways in which educators can teach vocabulary during reading.

Vocabulary on the Run

Identify particular words that need further instruction as you walk around and listen to the students read aloud with their buddies. Provide the meaning and examples right there on the spot, the instant that you know a student needs help with a word. To check for understanding, ask the student to give you a sentence with that word.

Sticky Notes

Provide students with sticky notes. Ask them to write down any words that they still have trouble understanding and to hand these to you as you walk by. Some teachers have a poster on a wall called a "parking lot" on which the students place the sticky notes. Remind them to first attempt to understand a word by discussing it with their buddy or looking it up in the glossary or dictionary. You can use these sticky notes to provide further explanations of words during or after the reading activity.

New Word / Maybe? / Yes!

In this exercise, students take notes in a table format (see table 6.5) during reading to keep track of unfamiliar words. They make note of a word in the first column and write what they think it means in the second. After reading, they go to a dictionary or consult others to write the appropriate meaning in the third column. Students can keep these notes in journal entries, in learning logs, in vocabulary banks, or on cards on a ring that will serve as personal dictionaries.

Table 6.5: The New Word / Maybe? / Yes! Exercise

New Word for Me	Maybe It Means . . .	Yes! This Is What It Means

Attempt the Context

This exercise is first modeled by the teacher. Once the strategy is internalized and working, students can apply this as a reflection process. While reading in pairs, students go through these steps when they encounter a difficult word or a sentence that does not make sense:

1. Ask, "What word in the sentence doesn't make sense?"

2. Read the sentence again, and the one before and the one after.

3. Change the word to an easy word you know. Does the sentence make sense now?

4. If you are still not sure, write the word in your learning log or on a sticky note.

These steps can be written on bookmarkers for a handy reference.

Teaching Vocabulary After Reading

After employing a strategy for teaching vocabulary, it is important to follow up with a debriefing. Debriefing helps students develop metalinguistic and metacognitive skills and become semantically aware. That is, students become more in tune and sensitive to the way they approach words and what works for them in learning those words.

Semantic awareness is a cognitive, metacognitive, affective, and linguistic stance toward words. Students who are word conscious are aware of the power of the words they read, hear, write, and speak. Semantic awareness helps students become more skillful and precise in word usage at high levels of complexity and sophistication (Calderón, 2009).

The school climate for vocabulary success described in the case study at the beginning of this chapter was created by teachers and administrators during semantic awareness meetings. They carefully planned and invented new ways of helping students learn words every day in every activity.

To teach the students the concept of semantic awareness, use a term and then, during the debriefing, ask students questions such as:

- What helped you remember the word?

- What will help you to not forget its meaning?

- How did you and your partner help each other when you didn't know a word?

- Who wants to share another semantic strategy?

At the end of the reading segment, even before you start a question-and-answer segment, conduct a "corners" or "go to the wall" activity. In a corners activity, students are asked to go to the four corners of the room and talk about the words that were introduced. You can post a different word at each corner, and students can choose the corner/word that they liked the most. Or, you can count off from one to four, and all the number ones go to one corner, the twos to another, and so on. In a go-to-the-wall activity, students stand along the wall in triads and each has thirty seconds to tell the other two how many words he or she remembers from the reading and preteaching of vocabulary.

Vocabulary Strategies

In addition to preteaching vocabulary and modeling vocabulary strategies during and after reading, other techniques can be planned for the week, some of which can be used as center activities. The following sections highlight some additional vocabulary strategies.

Integrated Strategies

Some vocabulary-building techniques that can be interspersed throughout the week's activities are:

- Labeling drawings and pictures to help students make the connection between oral and written English

- Creating a print-rich environment by displaying necessary vocabulary, concepts, and messages all over the classroom

- Using students' ideas, such as how to represent a character from a story, as a starting point and elaborating on them to clarify meaning (this allows the students to contribute to the process and enhances their self-esteem when their ideas are accepted)

- Incorporating role-playing activities to allow students to learn new concepts and language through personalized, physical activities, which give meaning to new vocabulary

Imagery

Visual images are a potent device in aiding recall of verbal material. This is particularly so for the large number of learners who have a preference for visual learning. The students are asked to draw or picture in their minds the meaning or an association or a sequence. Even the mental representation of the letters of a word is helpful.

Sounds of Cognates and False Cognates

At a listening/recording center, students are asked to identify a word in their own language that sounds like the new word. For example: *discussion* and *discusión*. This becomes an auditory link to meaning. The sound can also accompany a visual image to strengthen recall. However, some words may sound the same but not have the same meaning: *library* and *librería* (bookstore). Remind students that this exercise is only for sound and not meaning.

Acting Out

Students can physically act out a new expression such as *pouring poison into his ear, going into a frenzy,* and so forth. They can also relate a new expression to a feeling or sensation such as *freezing, lukewarm, heavy,* or *bumpy.* Abstract concepts such as *trial* and *betrayal* can be scripted out, rehearsed, and role-played.

Think Aloud

ELs need to pick up learning strategies and develop a plan to solve problems on their own. To help them with this, teachers or peer students say their thoughts aloud during decision making or an exercise. They describe their thoughts or actions step-by-step while doing the task and maybe even go back and state the whole procedure again. When their plan does not succeed, they can retrace their steps to investigate another way to solve the problem or improve on the product.

Read Aloud

When reading aloud to students, first preteach words you think they need to know using very simple language, pictures from the book, and brief self-questioning. Second, read the book once and then ask questions after reading. Third, reread the book, pausing to emphasize the words you pretaught and asking the children to repeat the word. Fourth, if you come to a word you know needs more explanation, do a think-aloud to elaborate on its meaning or give an example beyond the story. Fifth, ask more questions for the buddy pairs to discuss. Ask them to use the new words. Ask some to share using the new word(s).

Previewing a Selection

Teachers can introduce vocabulary while previewing a text with the students by:

- Writing additional key words on the board

- Asking students to read along

- Pointing to pictures in the book or to paragraphs where the words are found

- Discussing the title, pictures, and vocabulary in the context of the students' background knowledge

- Skimming to determine main ideas

- Scanning to find specific details of interest

Mapping After Reading

Semantic and cognitive maps are very effective in building vocabulary and concepts. Using semantic maps, webs, diagrams, or any graphic organizer engages students in a mental activity that activates prior knowledge and provides multidimensional contextual clues to the new vocabulary and concepts. It also gives ELs more vocabulary for talking about new knowledge or new words. First, model techniques for mapping on the board. Second, have small groups of students work on their maps. This preliminary practice will provide the ELs with patterns to replicate. Encourage students to use drawings for those words not yet in their repertoire.

Classifying After Reading

This technique is similar to mapping. Classifying vocabulary and concepts into meaningful units will make them easier to remember:

- Nouns, adjectives, or verbs

- Topics (words about plants or communities)

- Practical function (parts of the computer or joining words)

- Linguistic function (words for requesting, apologizing, demanding, or denying)

- Dissimilarity or opposition (friendly/unfriendly, dangerous/safe)

Words can be written on color-coded cards to represent the different groups. The cards can be used for cooperative learning activities during which students drill each other for meaning, concept mastery, or even spelling. These cards can also be kept in envelopes or on a ring or hung on strings from the ceiling for easy consultation during writing activities.

Foldables

Foldables are three-dimensional organizers that are useful for recording words, definitions, meaningful sentences, and representations of words. There are several different formats for foldables, including booklets, trifolds, and triangles. Visit http://cmase.pbworks.com/f/Foldable+Basics.pdf for examples of hot dog folds, hamburger folds, layered-look books, and shutter folds.

Highlighting

ELs sometimes benefit from highlighting vocabulary or key concepts with the help of other students or as a whole-group activity. There are several forms of highlighting:

- Dramatic use of color

- Underlining

- Bold type

- Italics

- Capital letters

- Initial capitals

- Big writing

- Stars

- Boxes

- Circles

- Shadows

- Dingbats

Quick Tips for Teaching Vocabulary

These quick tips offer some important reminders about vocabulary:

- Teach important words before reading, not after reading.

- Teach as many words as possible before, during, and after reading.

- Teach simple everyday words (tier 1 words), along with information-processing words (tier 2) and content-specific or academic words (tier 3).

- Use new words in the context of reading, talking, and writing within the same class period. Even level 1 students can begin reading and writing from day one.

- Point out lexical items (for example, tense, root, affixes, and phrasal and idiomatic uses) and use them as strategic learning tools.

- Require ELs to learn key words for a reading assignment and test that word knowledge at the end of the assignment.

- Avoid just sending ELs to look up words in the dictionary; they might select the wrong definition or just copy the meaning without understanding it.

- Don't expect ELs to figure out meaning from context without additional supports because there may be several other words they don't know in that context.

- Keep in mind that having a peer translate for an EL provides a quick answer but does not enable the student.

- Point out cognates and false cognates as a word-learning and spelling strategy.

- Require students to use new vocabulary in writing summaries of what has been learned on that topic.

Reflection Questions

The following questions are provided to initiate discussions on the topics and processes mentioned in this chapter.

For Teachers

1. How will you integrate the teaching of vocabulary into your lessons?

2. Can you provide more targeted vocabulary instruction in small groups or one-on-one?

3. What other activities will help develop semantic awareness in your students?

For Administrators

1. How can you promote semantic awareness throughout the school?

2. Do any of your teachers need additional professional development on vocabulary instruction for diverse students?

For Universities and Departments of Education

1. Are you preparing your teachers and administrators to teach vocabulary in a comprehensive way? If not, what else do you need to do?

2. How do your standards and teacher and student performance instruments dovetail with teaching and learning vocabulary?

CHAPTER SEVEN

Teaching Reading

ELs need decoding and fluency practice to become good readers—to recognize words and comprehend the text at the same time (Grabe, 2009; Nagy, 2005; Samuels, 1979). However, the greater the attention extended to decoding, the less there is available for comprehension. ELs need balanced time and attention for word meaning, decoding, grammatical structures, background knowledge, and comprehension skills.

Within its limitations, NCLB has managed to highlight the literacy needs of ELs. However, it has been a struggle. Programs such as Reading First reduced this attention to a few reading instructional strategies that were developed and tested for general education students. After Reading First programs were implemented, dissatisfaction with EL progress began to grow. The rush to get ELs on the same page as general education students resulted in pushbacks, not only for them, but also for the general education students.

Teachers were expected to record easily observable elements of reading, such as the number of words read in one minute, and to teach to the elements that were found on the state's tests. ELs learned to decode as quickly as possible, without understanding a word they were reading, in attempts to please the teacher. As Timothy Rasinski (2011), professor of literacy education at Kent State University, stated:

> Focusing on speed does not necessarily improve automaticity. Despite the flawed reasoning behind the use of rate as an instructional goal, we are now stuck with the so-called scientifically based approach to reading fluency that draws students' attention to speedy reading.

These practices caused ELs to fall further and further behind in developing depth of word knowledge and reading comprehension skills. They became bored with drills and continued to have difficulties with reading as they attempted to learn the content. Many ELs lost their love of reading in elementary school, and when they reached middle school, they were unmotivated struggling readers reading several grade levels below and still limited English proficient. These are the long-term ELs who populate the middle and high schools today.

Although Reading First was not effective for ELs, it did help to draw out more research on EL literacy, which has begun to point us in the right direction. For instance, we now know that primary language helps develop language and literacy in English and content reading helps to accelerate language and literacy.

Reading Skills and Processes

Reading is a linguistic and metalinguistic process for ELs. It is not possible to read without making graphemic-phonemic connections, without recognizing the words to be read and the structural phrases organizing the words, and without having a reasonable store of linguistic knowledge of the language of the text (Grabe, 2009).

It is easier for young children to learn to read in their primary language. When this is not possible and they have to learn to read in English, it is much harder for them. It is also much more difficult for their teachers because the linguistics, the lower-level processes of reading (phonemic awareness, decoding, fluency, working memory), and the higher-level processes of reading (comprehension processing, metacognitive awareness, content mastery) need to be intertwined for ELs to develop good reading skills. It's not an easy balancing act!

Learning to Read in the Primary Language

The National Literacy Panel on Language-Minority Children and Youth found that oral proficiency and literacy in the first language can be used to facilitate literacy development in English. Those who learn to read in their primary language are able to transfer some skills of reading to English (August, Calderón, & Carlo, 2001; August & Shanahan, 2008).

The majority of dual-language/bilingual programs teach ELs to read in their primary language before they transition to English reading around grade 2 or 3. Teachers often ask, "When is the best time to transition students to English? At second, third, or fourth grade?" The answer is, "When they have an academic vocabulary in Spanish [or other primary language] that is at grade level; their reading has reached automaticity in Spanish; they have mastered comprehension strategies for identifying cause and effect, sequencing, comparing, and contrasting; and they are able to write coherent paragraphs summarizing what they have read at grade level." Relying only on oral tests of language proficiency can be deceiving.

WHAT DOES THE RESEARCH SAY?

If students' vocabularies are too small, phonological awareness does not contribute to their knowledge about print. If students' levels of phonological awareness are too low, vocabulary does not contribute to their knowledge about print (Nagy, 2005).

The expectation that a short-term vocabulary intervention will produce large improvements in reading comprehension is simply not realistic; background knowledge, concepts and content, and generative word knowledge are necessary (Nagy, 2005).

Strategies for learning vocabulary and strategies for reading comprehension should not be taught separately but in the context of the text students are about to read (Calderón, 2009).

The purpose of culturally responsive instruction is to improve opportunities for academic success by letting student strengths and interests serve as a bridge to the new learning offered by the school (Au, 2009/2010).

Comprehension is influenced by text structures such as cause and effect or time-order relationships in nonfiction, the division of plays into acts and scenes, the rhyme and rhythm of poems, and dialogue in fiction (RAND Reading Study Group, 2002).

Being able to comprehend informational text is important because the texts that most adults read are informational (Duke & Pearson, 2002).

Informational text contributes to vocabulary growth and builds knowledge; it capitalizes on students' interests and curiosities, and provides valuable links to their own experiences (Duke & Pearson, 2002).

The National Literacy Panel on Language-Minority Children and Youth found that instruction that provides substantial coverage in the key components of reading identified by the National Reading Panel (phonemic awareness, phonics, fluency, vocabulary, and text comprehension) has clear benefits for language-minority students (August & Shanahan, 2006, 2008).

Schools that are able to implement dual-language programs do not have to worry about transition. Their students develop high levels of oracy and literacy skills in two languages at each grade level (Slavin & Cheung, 2005; Calderón & Carreón,

2001; Calderón & Minaya-Rowe, 2003).

Some language or literacy development guides are similar between English and Spanish, such as applying prefixes and suffixes, providing formal definitions, interpreting metaphors, developing reading comprehension strategies, spelling, and writing. But these features need to be pointed out and explicitly taught in order to become effective tools for bilingual children (Carlo et al., 2005).

Some languages, like Spanish, have a shallow orthography as compared to English—that is, sounds and spellings have a high correspondence. English has a lower correspondence between spelling and pronunciation. For example, the sound of "ch" in *chile* in Spanish is /ch/, and the English version of *chili* is also pronounced with a /ch/. However, English has several exceptions to the "ch" sound, as in *chef*, *chord*, *yacht*, *Charlotte*, and *echo*, whereas Spanish does not. These and many other inconsistent patterns of English make it difficult for students who are accustomed to high correlations of spelling and pronunciation.

The National Literacy Panel on Language-Minority Children and Youth (August & Shanahan, 2006) found that some reading skills easily transfer from one language to another. For instance, decoding and reading fluently are easier in English when ELs have learned to decode and read fluently in their primary language. This is why many ELs often keep pace with their English-speaking peers on fluency tests when the instructional focus was on decoding and fluency. However, the same ELs may not do well on reading comprehension and writing. For ELs to read and write proficiently in English, oral proficiency (word learning and grammatical understanding) in English is essential.

Higher-Order Reading Processes

Reading is basically a comprehension process. Comprehension strategies help students to relate ideas in a text to what they already know and make explicit what they don't know, to keep track of how well they understand what they read, and, when understanding breaks down, to identify what is causing the problem and how to solve it (Pressley, 1997). Strategy instruction is particularly important for ELs. Strategic knowledge helps ELs learn how to learn in a schooling system that is very new and perhaps very strange to them. ELs can benefit from figuring out the simplest book conventions and concepts of print and applying the more sophisticated strategies of selecting key information, organizing and mentally summarizing information, monitoring comprehension, and matching comprehension to teacher goals or test goals.

Preparing to Teach a Text

ELs need to read both fiction and nonfiction texts, as well as texts with different perspectives. Have on hand various sources of information throughout different genres. Materials should be selected to build essential information and also be of interest to the ELs. Once you have a text in mind, go through the following steps:

1. Determine desired outcomes for oracy, reading, and writing skills. How will you convey these to the ELs?

2. Identify the potential in texts for various instructional purposes, such as kinds of challenges a text would present to students—reading level, comprehension, cultural context—and text that can be handled by ELs.

3. Decide which vocabulary words to preteach so that ELs can understand and participate in the discussions, answer questions, and comprehend what they read.

4. Select questions for discussions.

5. Select ancillary materials to ensure comprehension of big ideas: real objects, pictures, websites, role-playing activities, gestures, or drawings.

6. Select a reading-comprehension or metacognitive strategy to model for the students, and plan how to model it.

7. Select the appropriate strategy to use in helping students produce writing.

8. Differentiate the level of scaffolding to provide different levels of support.

The more ELs read, the faster their vocabulary grows. The more vocabulary they have, the more eager they are to read. After they read and enjoy a good text, they want to write about it. Writing helps them learn more words. More words increase their vocabulary.

Reading Strategies

Reading is quite complex. The art of teaching reading has gone through years of iterations. Sometimes the emphasis is on decoding, sometimes fluency, and recently comprehension and word meaning. However, reading is not just fluency or comprehension or decoding. Reading is made up of several components: oral language proficiency, phonological processing, working memory, word-level skills, and text-level skills (August & Shanahan, 2008).

The National Reading Panel (2000) identified the most effective reading comprehension strategies: comprehension monitoring, using graphic and semantic organizers, using the structure of stories, answering questions, generating questions, and summarizing. Other researchers cite these comprehension strategies: predict, determine important information, summarize, make inferences, visualize, ask and answer questions, make connections, and monitor comprehension. Either set is useful in helping ELs develop strategies. However, ELs cannot be expected to make predictions or inferences or visualize if they don't know the words necessary to understand or express that prediction or inference or to visualize. A good foundation in word recognition, or decoding, is important because once ELs have automatic recognition of words (automaticity), they can focus more on the overall meaning. Comprehension calls for knowing 85–90 percent of the words in a sentence, a question, a paragraph, or any text.

Essentially, it is easier for ELs to begin with asking and answering questions, determining important information, summarizing, making connections and making use of schema, and monitoring comprehension. Such strategies should be applied immediately after they are modeled to reinforce the knowledge of the strategy and give teachers an opportunity to check the appropriate use of the strategy.

For ELs in beginning stages, the text to be read should be chunked into smaller segments than those being read by general education students. Students should be reading something different every day and engaged in greater analysis and application as they learn and apply new vocabulary, grammar, and writing. Repetitive reading of the same long passages does not help ELs develop fluency or comprehension. Worse, reading can become "*so* boring." Reading needs to be processed in smaller chunks in order to focus on strategy development. This is a great opportunity for guided practice. Don't worry about covering the material. It will get done. It goes slowly at first because students are learning to learn. Once they practice a strategy a few times, the whole process accelerates. When time isn't taken to develop metacognitive strategies, or learning how to learn, students get bogged down. Take your time if you want them to succeed.

Sentence Starters

Many times, ELs know the answer to a question but have difficulty figuring out how to start their response. Sentence starters help ELs articulate their ideas, responses, and explanations. The following sentence starters can help ELs in various types of academic discussion:

- **Summarizing**. Students create a new oral or written text that stands for an existing text. The summary contains the important information or big ideas.

  + This story tells about a . . .

  + This section is about the . . .

  + One important fact here is that . . .

- **Determining important information**. Students identify the most important idea in a section of text, distinguishing it from details that tell more about it.

  + The main idea is . . .

  + The key details that support that are . . .

  + The purpose of this text is to . . .

- **Sequencing**. Students make sense of the order in which ideas are presented to enhance comprehension.

  + The first step in this experiment is . . .

  + The sequence for answering this math problem is . . .

  + The first thing the character did was . . . Next, the character . . .

- **Making connections, visualizing, or creating schema**. Students practice relating new information to prior knowledge from their own culture or schooling. They create images to make connections between texts and their own lives and the world. They create schema when teachers model a variety of these strategies.

  + This reminds me of the time when I . . .

  + My parents told me a story about . . .

  + I read in another book that . . .

Some teachers glue these prompts on folders and arrange them as tents in the middle of the tables when students are working in teams. Students can practice a couple of examples per week. As teachers monitor discussions, they might want to give extra points to those who use the examples consistently.

Content-Focused Instruction

Literature is probably one of the most difficult subjects for ELs. There are too many variations of author's language, metaphors, idioms, Anglicisms, and registers. Science, on the other hand, is a language that is more precise, more structured and consistent, and has many cognates. Math and social studies also have many cognates. Literature has very few cognates because most words are Anglo-Saxon derivatives (for example, *troll, bunny, itsy bitsy spider, plot, setting, foreshadowing*).

Introducing reading through subject-area content in the early grades has an added benefit for ELs. They learn important facts that lay a foundation for math, science, and social studies while they learn vocabulary and reading skills. Math, science, social studies, and language arts have their own unique genre structures. The way a student should read a science book is very different from how he or she should read a math problem, and that is quite different from the way he or she should read a poem or piece of literature, which in turn changes considerably when the student reads current events or history. The way to approach reading and writing in each of these subjects is most likely quite different from the way ELs have typically been asked to read and write in an ESL class. Therefore, it is important to teach students "how to read" the different subject domains. The good news for teachers is that all students benefit from reading through the content areas, and the process for teaching reading through different subject domains is basically the same as teaching reading with literature.

Teacher Modeling

Chapters 5 and 6 discussed the importance of preteaching the words that will help students derive meaning from the text. That is the first step in building comprehension. Next, teachers should consider modeling. The sequence for modeling reading comprehension is as follows:

1. The teacher models how to deconstruct each sentence, with a student, in order to construct meaning.

2. The teacher reads aloud and thinks aloud to model a comprehension strategy.

3. Students are asked to apply the deconstruction strategy and the comprehension strategy.

4. The teacher models how to summarize what they have learned after each paragraph using the new words.

5. Students read with their buddies, alternating sentences, and summarize after each paragraph.

6. The teacher monitors by walking around the classroom, recording students' use of strategies as they conduct partner reading.

For example, in the following passage, the teacher's think-alouds for monitoring comprehension are in brackets:

> There's lots of evidence of drastic changes {*big changes*} in climate occurring in the distant past. {*We know a lot about many changes in climate that have happened in the past.*} Earth today may again be in the midst {*in the middle*} of such a climate change. {*Today, there are many changes happening again.*} In the last one hundred years, studies show that {*people have studied these changes and they can show us that*} global temperatures {*temperatures around the world*} have risen {*have gone up*} an average of 0.6 degrees C. {*What is that "C"? Is it centigrade; is it centimeter? I'm not sure. My reading partner isn't sure either. I better ask my teacher. I'm going to put this on a sticky note and put the sticky note on the parking lot so that my teacher can explain this to us.*}

This teacher substituted easier words for some of the words, indicating that the students can also do their think-alouds with easy words. Showing students that even teachers don't know everything and that they ask for help after they have tried figuring it out is a way of reassuring the students that it is all right to get help. After modeling, the teacher asks the students to read a paragraph with their reading buddy and deconstruct it sentence by sentence to make sure they understand what they are reading.

The next day, the teacher conducts think-alouds to model comprehension strategies, such as summarizing, finding cause and effect or main idea, or sequencing. For example, the teacher reads a paragraph aloud and then summarizes it at the end. Alternatively, with the help of a student, the teacher models how to read alternating sentences and summarize at the end of each paragraph. She emphasizes that this time, instead of deconstructing, the students are actually constructing quality sentences using as many of the new words as possible. She reminds students that this is the time to activate that working memory that has stored the new words.

When modeling reading aloud, demonstrate and elaborate on many of the important subtle techniques—such as pronunciation of words and dramatic voice inflection—that add meaning and emotion to the written word. Model how to ask comprehension questions or think aloud while reading so the students can apply metacognitive devices during their silent reading (for example, fix-it strategies, purpose for reading, finding main idea, summarizing a few sentences).

Partner Reading

Partner reading and summarizing is critically important for ELs while reading math, science, and social studies. It helps students understand and learn the content areas. There are several options for partner reading approaches. Those that call for students to alternate reading sentences aloud with a partner are most effective with ELs. One option is for the first student to read a sentence and do a think-aloud; he or she is then followed by the second student, who reads the next sentence and does a think-aloud. Another is to alternate reading each sentence aloud (without the think-aloud), followed by both peers talking about what they read after each paragraph.

Reading only one sentence at a time helps them to approach reading in smaller chunks and gives them more confidence. It also keeps both partners on task. They have to listen to each other because there is no time for distraction. Students can get distracted or bored or wander off mentally when their buddy is reading a whole paragraph, especially if the buddy is a struggling reader. Alternating sentences keeps both alert and listening to one another. Having to summarize what they read after each paragraph helps even further.

While students are partner reading, walk from pair to pair and catch them doing something right. Record a strategy they used, the application of new words, fluency, or extended discourse. Use your notes to later give feedback to the students or to share the progress with their parents.

Ten minutes of daily partner reading for each subject area will yield dramatic improvements in reading for all students. ELs can reread independently at another time. Partner reading is more effective than silent reading because the students get to hear themselves read and discuss the content to be mastered with a buddy. They can test their ideas and second-language efforts in a safe context. It is most effective immediately after the teacher models, when the strategy and the flow of the narrative are fresh in their minds.

Silent reading following partner reading helps students reinforce their reading skills and anchor their understanding. Since it will then be familiar reading, they will feel accomplished and enjoy reading. When they are asked to read silently the first time a text is introduced, the fear of failure or embarrassment makes it difficult for them to plow through by themselves. Silent reading doesn't help ELs if vocabulary instruction and partner reading have not preceded it.

Sponge Activities After Reading

While employing the partner reading strategy, some pairs will finish reading and discussing before others. Have a list of enrichment or sponge activities to soak up the time. Post them on chart paper or distribute them on cards for these pairs. Maybe they earn an extra point for each? Here are some examples of what the partners can do:

- Discuss what they learned.

- Map out main ideas or critical elements.

- Find meanings of words they don't know.

- Work on their word banks.

- Give each other pretests and practice the answers missed.

- Work on the pronunciation of new words.

- Write in their journals or learning logs.

Choral Reading

Choral reading can be conducted in several ways: the whole class reads aloud together with the teacher; the teacher reads a sentence or paragraph, and the class reads the following sentence or paragraph together; one student table reads together, then another; half the class reads, then the other half; and so forth. Choral reading is beneficial when the teacher is presenting a new text, particularly if the new text has features and structures that are different from the text the students have been accustomed to reading. This strategy helps all students practice pronunciation and prosody. However, teachers should use choral reading for only three to five minutes per subject area per day to leave time for the other types of reading.

Example Literacy Block

During the ExC-ELL project, researchers worked with teachers to test ways to introduce ELs to a full range of reading skills and different types and levels of vocabulary, to build fluency, and to ensure that students master the concepts and content they are reading (Calderón, 2007a, 2007b; Calderón & Minaya-Rowe, 2011). These researchers among others (Calderón, Ford, Raphael, & Teale, 2010) propose implementing language and literacy components in five phases for a balanced literacy approach that can address diverse reading levels of students. They propose the literacy block as shown in figure 7.1.

Teachers like to use this format because they get to work with both the whole class and small groups for differentiation. Students can be reading at three or four different levels on the same topic, learning the same vocabulary. (Publishers such as the Wright Group LEAD21 and Benchmark Education Company produce books on the same themes but at different readability levels.) The literacy block is effective for differentiating, accelerating, and providing equity in literacy. Following is an example of a ninety-minute literacy block using the model in figure 7.1 but adapted for effective instruction for ELs.

During the first thirty minutes of the ninety-minute literacy block, second-grade teacher Mrs. Ramos introduces the tier 1, 2, and 3 vocabulary words that she selected from the texts the students are about to read; the vocabulary words range from easy to sophisticated to content-specific words dealing with ecosystems. Mrs. Ramos presents steps 1 through 5 (see chapter 6) of vocabulary instruction for each word. Turning to their left-elbow buddies, the students interact to practice vocabulary step 6: applying each new word in different contexts. After twelve minutes, the teacher reminds the students that these words are the vocabulary objective of the day and that she wants to see them written from memory on their exit passes (see chapter 9) at the end of the ninety minutes. Mrs. Ramos explains that the content objective is to learn about animals that live in these different ecosystems, and the reading comprehension strategy is finding examples of cause and effect. She highlights a grammatical structure (a compound sentence) for step 7 of vocabulary instruction and mentions that this week they will be studying compound sentences and using them in their writing. She uses the SMART Board to show photographs of the ecosystems they will be reading about and the flowers and animals that live in each to build some background knowledge. Using a think-aloud strategy with one of the books, she models thinking about text features and structures and finding an example of cause and effect. Her timer goes off, indicating the thirty minutes are up; it is time to move to student practice.

After Mrs. Ramos finishes her whole-group instruction, the students go to their desks, which are configured for teams of four. Each table has four books that are the same and at the same readability level. Mrs. Ramos has twenty-four students

WHOLE-GROUP Interactive Reading

All students learn the same concepts, theme vocabulary, and literacy skills.

SMALL-GROUP Differentiated Reading

Students work with the teacher in small groups, using carefully crafted connected text sets (same topic, same key vocabulary, same covers, different readability levels).

INDEPENDENT Application and Practice

Students practice and extend skills and strategies with peers, online, and in reading centers.

WHOLE-GROUP Cross-Text Sharing

Students build on what they learned through cross-text sharing, inquiry projects, and cooperative learning activities. Small mixed groups share unique content from the differentiated readers and work on inquiry projects.

WHOLE-GROUP Writing and Language Arts

Students learn grammar and mechanics, and fully participate in all aspects of the writing process.

INDEPENDENT Writing or **TEAM** Writing

WHOLE-GROUP Inquiry and Wrap-Up

The whole class reconvenes to share what they have learned and produced, to make text connections, and to participate in assessment.

Figure 7.1: A balanced literacy approach.

Source: Adapted from Calderón, Ford, Raphael, & Teale, 2010.

reading at four levels. Four students are newcomers reading at a K–1 level; eight students are at level 1.5; eight are at level 2; and four are at an advanced level ranging from 2.5 to 3.5. Although the students are sitting in teams of four, they read in pairs using readers at their level. The teacher walks around to monitor for quality reading, use of new vocabulary, and application of comprehension strategies. This helps her target the needs of students for the small-group instruction that will follow this phase. It is also an opportunity to use her observation protocol and record the progress of her two lowest and two highest readers. Tomorrow, she will observe and record four of her students at class level. Each day, she records different students; when she has gone through the whole class, she starts all over again.

After twelve minutes, she calls her K–1 group over to work with them on additional vocabulary and decoding skills for the next twenty minutes. The other teams of four are rereading, summarizing orally what they read, and mapping the information using graphic organizers. Each team has a different ecosystem, and they will present information about their ecosystem to the whole class; they must also formulate two questions to ask the other teams after they present their information. Each student must do one-quarter of the presentation. The ELs, who are reading their K–1 ecosystem book with the teacher's assistance, will need to go back after twenty minutes and work on their presentation and graphic organizer.

After twenty minutes, the teacher asks another team of four to work with her. The ELs work on their presentation; the other students are on the computers reading e-books, doing some e-activities, or completing e-assessments.

When the teacher is finished with the small-group instruction, she addresses the whole group again. Mrs. Ramos has about two hundred single-copy books in her classroom library. She reminds students to take one home for the week; read it with parents, siblings, or caretakers; and bring a note on Friday confirming it was read at home. Toward the end of the period, she collects exit passes.

What does the rest of the week look like?

On day 2, for the first ten minutes, Mrs. Ramos introduces new tier 1, 2, and 3 words using the seven steps. She asks students to spend ten minutes doing partner reading of the second part of the book, alternating sentences and taking turns retelling what they learned after each paragraph. She monitors the retelling.

Then, for the next ten minutes, she highlights and discusses features of expository text structures. She asks students to integrate tier 2 and 3 words into their writing objective for the week: using cause and effect and the editing strategy of eliminating unnecessary repetition. Since this is the beginning of the year, she distributes a sheet listing sentence starters and connectors—for example, *in addition* and *in conclusion*. The students will be assigned a cooperative writing project, so she reviews the card of social protocols that students have on their desks, explaining how to interrupt politely, question, and reach consensus. She proceeds to explain the writing activity.

The thirty-minute writing segment begins with team prewriting as Mrs. Ramos guides the students through the writing activity, followed by an editing strategy. All students work with cooperative learning strategies that support discussions about the text with particular oral strategies (for example, recall, paraphrasing, summarization, question formulation, and sentence starter frames).

Teams spend the last thirty minutes working on their graphic organizers, formulating questions, and rehearsing for their presentations. Some are on the computers reading or working on e-activities or e-assessments. Toward the end of the period, Mrs. Ramos collects exit passes.

Days 3 and 4 are repeats of the day 1 schedule. Mrs. Ramos explicitly teaches more vocabulary with the seven steps, provides more explicit instruction and modeling of another comprehension skill, "making inferences," that dovetails with cause and effect. She works with two other groups for twenty minutes each. Students work on their writings and their presentations.

Day 5 is a day of celebration. Students present their graphic organizers and the information they learned about their ecosystems. They pose their questions to the other teams before and after each presentation. This helps the other teams stay focused on the information and encourages them to write down some key words while listening in order to be able to answer the questions. After forty minutes of presentations, applause, and celebrations, Mrs. Ramos explains what *inquiry* and *research* mean. She spends fifteen minutes showing examples on the SMART Board and asking students to "put their heads together" and start to think about what kind of research they would like to do next week on ecosystems. She shows some of the research and products from the previous year's students and gets them excited about what they can accomplish.

The next twenty minutes are spent celebrating the writing masterpieces of each team. Students share their well-edited stories and some creative decorations made out of construction paper.

Mrs. Ramos spends the last fifteen minutes debriefing the students and collecting their exit passes, the classroom library books they took home for independent reading, and the notes signed by parents that they read the book at home.

Since performance assessments and monitoring of student progress are conducted during every activity, traditional tests can be conducted on day 5 every two weeks or so. Types of daily assessments can include: observation and documentation of students using new vocabulary, of fluency during partner reading, or of social, cooperative, or behavioral skills during partner and team activities; reading inventories during team activities; rubrics and team and individual products focusing on the use of tier 2 and 3 words, question formulation, and presentation or oral discourse.

Following is another example of time allocations for the ninety-minute literacy block:

- Five minutes for the introduction of tasks and goals, objectives, or expected outcomes

- Ten minutes for preteaching vocabulary

- Ten minutes for background building

- Ten minutes for modeling the reading comprehension skill to be applied

- Ten minutes for partner reading and summarizing

- Ten minutes for a whole-group discussion or activity

- Ten minutes for basic reading and writing skills

- Ten minutes for writing

- Ten minutes for anchoring what the students have learned thus far

- Five minutes for writing exit passes

Teachers who only have forty-five or sixty minutes can stop where time runs out and pick up where they left off the next day.

Some teachers look at this schedule and say, "But you only have ten minutes here for reading!" Myths have emerged from past teaching practices and beliefs about reading—such as, a teacher needs to read aloud to children for half the period, students should spend half the period reading silently, and teachers should model a reading strategy for half the period and have students use that strategy during their silent reading. The ten-minute formula actually enables more student reading, practice and application of reading comprehension skills, and better content connections.

Grammar, Syntax, and Pronunciation

Students learn grammatical and syntactic features such as prepositional phrases, spelling, tense, compound sentences, and passive voice faster when the teacher points them out in the text the students are reading. There are differences between sound/symbol and syntactic/structural relationships to keep in mind while teaching Spanish speakers to read in English.

For instance, in Spanish, vowels have only one sound and one way of writing that sound. English has about fifteen different vowel sounds and numerous combinations of vowels. How many different vowel sounds can you count in the following words?

> peat, pit, pate, pet, pat, putt, pert, pooh, put, Poe, paw, par

> beet, bit, bait, bet, bat, bite, but, bought, bottle, boot, boat, boy, bow

ELs may have pronunciation difficulties with:

- Vowel digraph combinations—*ou, ow, eigh, all, au, aw, oo*

- Consonant blends—*sl, sm, st, scr, spr, str*

- Consonant digraphs—*th, wh, ph*; the differences between these digraphs: *sh, ch* (ship, chip; share, chair; Shirley, Chuck)

- Initial sounds—*kn, qu, wr*

- Final sounds—*ck, ng, gh*

- Variations of the "-ed" endings—crawled, walked, sprinted

- Variations of the "–s" endings—pats, classes, welcomes

Some syntactic structures may also cause difficulties:

- Compound sentences or chunks of words that contain long noun phrases— *when it rains, we have to wear our raincoats, boots, and . . .*

- Compound words—*playground, sidewalk, trash can, blackboard*

- Connectors or prepositional phrases—*next, besides, is . . . than, if . . . then, since, nevertheless, in spite of, according to, at home, in time*

- Collocations or phrasal verbs and institutionalized units—*not yet, have a nice day, certainly, I see your point but . . . , as far as I know, see ya*

- Passive voice structures—*The two biggest mortgage lenders were rescued by the government* versus *The government rescued the two biggest mortgage lenders.*

In addition to tense, punctuation, and part of speech, syntactic structures can be taught from the context of what the students are about to read. Grammar is the basis of tying core concepts together in textbooks and in discourse. Students need to practice talking about cause and effect, classification, inferences, compare/contrast, descriptions of events and processes, and so forth—in other words, all the functions that nest the core standards and core concepts to be learned. Students also need explicit instruction and examples from the texts they are reading on: compound sentences, connectors, prepositional phrases, noun phrases, verbal phrases, figurative language, metaphors, similes, idioms, passive voice structures, variation in tense, clusters, and less familiar text structures.

Balancing Strategy Instruction

Strategy instruction sometimes causes students to devote too much of their time and thinking to the features of strategies at the expense of getting meaning from texts (Murphy & Alexander, 2000). Sometimes teachers make strategy instruction more complicated than the reading selection (Pearson & Fielding, 1991). Strategy instruction for ELs must be handled with care. They will benefit from explicit explanations of some key strategies for finding cause and effect, comparing/contrasting, and problem solving, particularly those newcomers who have limited literacy skills in their primary language. But as Beck and others recommend, this should not be the whole focus of reading—again, it's the art of balancing, balancing, balancing!

Quick Tips for Teaching Reading

These quick tips offer some important reminders about teaching reading:

- Preteach key vocabulary and discussion prompts such as sentence starters.

- Focus on comprehension before speed and decoding.

- Engage in explicit reading instruction before partner reading.

- Assign partner reading before silent or independent reading.

- Use center activities to help anchor vocabulary and reading objectives or comprehension strategies.

- Use the same reading approach for subject-matter reading.

- Model, model, model!

- Have sponge activities handy for partner reading, writing, and center activities.

- Keep the literacy block balanced and moving briskly.

Reflection Questions

The following questions are provided to initiate discussions on the topics and processes mentioned in this chapter.

For Teachers

1. What aspects of the reading process described in this chapter are you implementing?

2. Which parts have you been leaving out and will now include?

3. Does your collection of texts cut across all subject areas and all genres? Are the texts interesting and challenging enough for ELs?

For Administrators

1. How will you support your teachers as they integrate more instructional strategies for developing language and literacy into all subject areas?

2. How will you balance your budget allocations to provide quality professional development and to purchase great materials (in both languages if you have a dual-language program)?

3. As you observe teachers integrate language and literacy, what instructional features do you consider to be most important?

For Universities and Departments of Education

1. How can you assist departments of math, science, and social studies in integrating language and literacy instruction in their courses?

2. Do your guidelines for EL instruction reflect a thorough approach to academic vocabulary and reading comprehension at the elementary level?

CHAPTER EIGHT

Teaching Writing

The next step in the instructional sequence is writing, both small pieces about what is being learned every day and summative pieces to end the week or unit. Writing is the most difficult domain for ELs and their teachers. ELs need to develop writing skills for each content area as they simultaneously learn, comprehend, and apply content-area concepts through the second language (Garcia & Godina, 2004; Genesee, Lindholm-Leary, Saunders, & Christian, 2005; Graham & Perin, 2007). They also need to practice language mechanics and editing in content-area projects and build portfolios that include academic writing.

Writing cannot be taught as a "writing unit" totally separate from what the students have been reading and learning. Such mini lessons in writing sometimes become an end in themselves, devoid of context or continuity in learning. Just as phonics alone was detrimental to ELs for so many years, meaningless mini writing lessons can be just as much a waste of time. Writing should be engaging for each student. Story-related writing or content summaries, concept descriptions, and concept personifications help students not only apply patterns they have read but also remember the concepts or literature characteristics they are reading about.

Writing Strategies

A report commissioned by the Carnegie Corporation of New York, *Writing Next*, identifies eleven instructional practices that improve the quality of writing for students in grades 4 through 12: self-regulated strategy development, summarization, collaborative writing, specific product goals, word processing, sentence combining, prewriting, inquiry activities, process writing approach, study of models, and writing for content learning (Graham & Perin, 2007). Unfortunately, the report does not include data or research on effective writing for ELs; none of the studies focused on ELs. Nevertheless, these are some very promising strategies that may be adapted for ELs.

WHAT DOES THE RESEARCH SAY?

Seventy percent of students in grades 4–12 are low-achieving writers (Persky, Daane, & Jin, 2003).

Eighty percent of white- and blue-collar workers need writing skills (Graham & Hebert, 2010).

Nearly one-third of high school graduates are not ready for college-level English composition courses (ACT, 2005).

Most jobs today require writing skills, and private companies spend billions annually on remediation (National Commission on Writing, 2005).

For ELs, vocabulary knowledge, reading, and writing are connected and must be practiced in all the disciplines (National Research Council, 2010).

Learning logs, journals, and exit passes are effective ways for students to write about what they are learning (Atwell, 1998).

Self-Regulated Strategy Development

Explicitly teaching strategies for planning, writing, and editing has a strong impact on the quality of students' writing, especially those who have difficulty. One such approach is self-regulated strategy development, shown in figure 8.1.

This instructional practice appears to be the most comprehensive of the eleven identified by the researchers. It also lends itself to expanding to meet the needs of ELs. The teacher scaffolds all the elements from building background to providing words and text models for writing. The only thing not covered in this strategy is modeling continuously throughout the writing. Tell the students to use as many tier 2 and tier 3 words as possible and to count how many they have actually used.

Students in proficiency levels 1 and 2 or in grades K–2 will benefit from reading easier books with shorter sentences. Point out simple noun-verb-object combinations, adjectives before nouns, and punctuation. Their writing can consist of three or four sentences. Students in proficiency levels 3 to 5 or in grades 3–5 can read books with compound sentences and clauses. After pointing these out, as well as the use of compound words, adverbs, and basic sentence structures, instruct the

Self-regulated strategy development (SRSD) is an approach for planning, drafting, and revising text. It is characterized by explicit teaching, individualized instruction, and criterion-based versus time-based learning. Children are treated as active collaborators in the learning process. Instruction takes place in six stages:

1. **Develop background knowledge**. Students are taught any background knowledge needed to use the strategy successfully.

2. **Describe it**. The strategy and its purpose and benefits are described and discussed.

3. **Model it**. The teacher models how to use the strategy.

4. **Memorize it**. The student memorizes the steps of the strategy and any accompanying mnemonic.

5. **Support it**. The teacher supports or scaffolds student mastery of the strategy.

6. **Use it independently**. Students use the strategy with few or no supports.

Students are also taught a number of self-regulation skills (including goal setting, self-monitoring, self-instruction, and self-reinforcement) designed to help them manage writing strategies, the writing process, and their behavior. Mnemonics are introduced to help students remember strategies to increase performance. Two such strategies are PLAN and WRITE.

PLAN

P—Pay attention to the prompt.

L—List the main idea.

A—Add supporting ideas.

N—Number your ideas.

WRITE

W—Work from your plan to develop your thesis statements.

R—Remember your goals.

I—Include transition words for each paragraph.

T—Try to use different kinds of sentences.

E—Exciting, interesting $10,000 words.

Figure 8.1: Self-regulated strategy development.

Sources: Adapted from De La Paz & Graham, 2002; Harris & Graham, 1996; and Calderón, in press.

students to practice writing four or five sentences for accuracy. After several accurate attempts, they can move on to longer and more sophisticated structures and styles.

Summarization

Summarization involves "explicitly and systematically teaching students how to summarize texts" (Graham & Perin, 2007). Summarization is an effective language function and reading comprehension skill that needs to be used in writing. When ELs have been explicitly taught sentence starters for summarization, they can transfer these into their writing. Examples of sentence starters include:

- The author is writing about . . .

- The author is comparing . . . with . . .

- Three facts I learned are (1) . . . , (2) . . . , (3) . . .

- First of all, . . .

- One important thing is . . .

- We read about . . . and discovered . . .

Collaborative Writing

In collaborative writing assignments, students work together to plan, draft, revise, and edit their compositions. Collaborative writing—or cooperative writing, as it is sometimes called—is a great tool for ELs. Planning, drafting, writing, and editing in pairs or teams enrich language and ideas.

Specific Product Goals

The specific product goals strategy calls for students to be assigned "specific, reachable goals for the writing they are to complete" (Graham & Perin, 2007). Graham and Perin offer as an example the writing of a persuasive letter as a goal. They also recommend that teachers provide "explicit subgoals on argumentative discourse, including a statement of belief, two or three reasons for that belief, examples or supporting information for each reason, two or three reasons why others might disagree, and why those reasons are incorrect" (Graham & Perin, 2007). This example might work with more advanced ELs if they have models for each element suggested. Beginning ELs will need to start with simple letter writing, then gradually work up to persuasive letter writing. Argumentative discourse can be introduced after extensive practice with the first two assignments.

Word Processing

Word processing "uses computers and word processors as instructional supports for writing assignments" (Graham & Perin, 2007). Typing text on the computer with word-processing software will allow ELs to see their writing in a neat format; it is also easy to add, delete, use spell-check, look up words in the dictionary, and/or add pictures where they lack words. Computers also facilitate cooperative writing.

Sentence Combining

Sentence combining "involves teaching students to construct more complex, sophisticated sentences" (Graham & Perin, 2007). When sentence combining is taught in the context of what the students are reading, it is a better alternative to teaching an isolated grammar lesson. ELs can begin by using connectors such as *and*, *but*, and *because*. As they become more advanced, they will understand the concept of sentence combining as they practice embedding different types of clauses and phrases.

Prewriting

Prewriting "engages students in activities designed to help them generate or organize ideas for their compositions" (Graham & Perin, 2007). Graphic organizers are typically used to draft or map out ideas before writing. However, using graphic organizers or brainstorming for ELs may not be the best way to start writing. ELs need substantial guidance in graphing ideas. When brainstorming requires rapid responses, ELs are at a disadvantage because they need time to pull their thoughts together into sentences. By then, the class or the group has moved on to another topic. Graphic organizers can be introduced for the summarization of ideas at first. Then, after students have grasped the concept, others can be introduced for prewriting.

Inquiry Activities

Inquiry activities engage students in "analyzing immediate, concrete data to help them develop ideas and content for a particular writing task" (Graham & Perin, 2007). For example:

> Students examine and infer the qualities of a number of objects in order to describe them in writing. The students touch objects while wearing

blindfolds, examine seashells, listen to sounds, do physical exercise, become more aware of bodily sensations, examine pictures, pantomime brief scenarios, act out dialogues, and examine model compositions. Students' responses to these objects are elicited. Students list more and more precise details, and respond to each other's descriptions in small groups or whole classes under teacher guidance in order to become increasingly aware of the writing task and possible audience reactions to the written product. (Graham & Perin, 2007)

This is a good prewriting and writing activity for K–3 ELs if it is accompanied by labels that describe what the students have just touched, smelled, or experienced. For example, a chart similar to table 8.1 can be displayed or given to the students with words that have been part of the lesson.

Table 8.1: Recap of Words and Phrases

Nouns	Adjectives	Verbs	Useful Phrases
rabbit	hard	flow	sounds like
flower	soft	move	smells like
rocks	fluffy	sink	feels like
seeds	rough	avoid	reminds me of
	sweet	carry	there was a
	strong	hide	if you see one

Process Writing Approach

The process writing approach—that is, drafting, writing, editing, and publishing—"interweaves a number of writing instructional activities in a workshop environment that stresses extended writing opportunities, writing for authentic audiences, personalized instruction, and cycles of writing" (Graham & Perin, 2007). Process writing and writing workshops are not as effective as one would think, particularly with ELs, as process writing can be difficult to manage when there is a wide range of students. ELs will benefit from process writing or writing workshops when they contain elements of those strategies that seem to work better (for example, study of models, inquiry, sentence combining, writing to learn, collaborative or cooperative writing) and, most important, when vocabulary is pretaught and students read good models of texts that contain the elements teachers want to see in their writing.

Study of Models

Modeling is perhaps one of the best ways to introduce quality writing to ELs. Providing one brief well-written simple piece each week for students to emulate will help ELs eventually begin to experiment with different genres (for example, letter writing, stories, poems, expository writing). Ask students to highlight the connectors, sentence starters, punctuation, and other features in the model, then to apply some of the same features to their own writing.

Types of writing can be modeled and explained by the teacher on an overhead or SMART Board. Teachers can also provide ELs with charts, such as table 8.2, that can help them remember purposes and key phrases. The students can add more phrases as they discover them.

Table 8.2: Modeling Aid

Writing Mode	Purpose	Key Verbs/Phrases
Descriptive/Expressive	Use concrete or sensory details to describe a person, place, or event so that readers can visualize and sense what is described.	describe, create a picture
Narrative	Tell a story (real, personal, or imaginary) in a time sequence.	tell, tell about a time, imagine that
Expository/Informative	Convey information by explaining ideas, facts, or processes, without analysis or interpretation.	explain, explain how, tell why (cause and effect), classify, compare and contrast
Persuasive	Influence or convince the reader to agree with the writer by providing reasons or examples.	convince, persuade, present an argument about an idea or point of view

Writing for Content Learning

Writing for content learning "uses writing as a tool for learning content material" (Graham & Perin, 2007). Because writing in the content areas is one of the most demanding tasks in middle schools and high schools, it is important for elementary school teachers to assign more content writing or writing for content mastery (for example, main point and supporting evidence, biographies, lab reports, inquiry research reports, essays, persuasive writing). Fifth-grade students need to be prepared to undertake writing such as:

- Expository writing patterns that include presenting a main point and supporting it with concrete evidence

- Expository writing that is contingent on the ability to analyze and explain

- Expository writing that shows relationships between ideas and concepts

- Expository writing that involves making a claim or taking a position while supporting it with details and evidence

- Expository writing that uses a logical organization with complex sentence structures and connectors

Collaborative Writing, Revising, and Editing

Writing doesn't have to be a chore. Fun and effective learning activities for drafting, writing, revising, and editing will engage all students in the writing process. The writing strategies described in the following sections can be used to generate interest and get all students started on their writing.

Write-Around

For this strategy, it is best to have students sitting in teams of four. In the cooperative learning activity write-around (or *carrusel* in Spanish), after reading, the teacher assigns a sentence starter, such as "Yesterday we went to the zoo and . . . ," to capture the concepts and vocabulary that the students just read about. The teacher also reminds the students to use as many tier 2 and 3 words as possible. Students clear their desks, except for a piece of paper and a pencil. Each student copies the prompt on a sheet of paper, completes the sentence, and passes the paper to the right. The next student reads what was written, writes another sentence, and then passes the paper to the right. Students must read the previously written sentences and add another sentence to each paper he or she receives. This procedure is followed until the teacher calls time.

Each student reads the composition he or she is holding to the team and then selects the one he or she likes best. This is the one that the student will revise and edit.

The students add an introduction that will hook the reader, write a conclusion appropriate to the genre and purpose of the composition, review the paper for errors in spelling and/or conventions, add more tier 2 and tier 3 words where possible, and reread the improved composition aloud to their group.

Stretch and Grow

The "stretch and grow" exercise adds more adjectives or adverbs, tier 2 and 3 words, and embedded phrases to a student's writing; ELs can continuously "grow their sentences." For example, a simple sentence such as "I like the character" could be stretched to include more details: "I found that character to be very exciting because she was not afraid."

Expanding simple sentences in this way allows for continuous growth in language development. This type of language development contributes not only to students' conversational and social learning but also to their academic learning (Rydland & Aukrust, 2005).

Cut and Grow

Jeanne Cantu, a teacher trainer who specializes in writing for ELs, asks students to use the "cut and grow" activity to elaborate on a written composition, make it richer and more exciting, and use more sophisticated language. This revision technique helps students layer and bring depth to their writing.

Students need the following supplies:

- Their compositions

- A blank sheet of paper, preferably another color

- Scissors

- Tape

Students are given the following instructions:

1. Find a sentence in the composition that lacks specificity and detail. Do not choose the first or last sentence in a paragraph.

2. Add information to the sentence that will enhance or give depth to the idea. Use more tier 2 and tier 3 words. For example, the original sentence from a first-draft composition is: *The price of gas is high.* The elaborated sentence/idea is: *Gas is so expensive that I can only afford to put in $15 at a time. I used*

to let my brother borrow my car and wouldn't worry about the gas. Now I make him pay me every time he uses it.

3. Write the elaborated sentence on the colored sheet of paper.

4. Cut the composition right below the original sentence and tape it onto the colored sheet. Then, tape the rest of the composition to the colored sheet.

Students can immediately see how their papers have "grown" and been improved through this revision strategy.

Too Many Repetitions?

Students need colored markers, pencils, or crayons for this activity. The teacher asks the students to create a chart like table 8.3. The students then check their papers for an overuse of "to be" verbs and sentences beginning with *the*. In this way, students can check for repetition. All the sentences in a paragraph might begin with *the*, but the student might not be aware of this until a rectangle is placed around that word. Once the student counts the number of times he or she used *the*, he or she has an option of varying sentence beginnings. This strategy also teaches sentence reconstruction and the use of more sophisticated words.

Teachers may need to do a mini lesson beforehand to ensure students' understanding, and they should start by checking for one type of correction per paper and add more as the students learn the process.

Table 8.3: Too Many Repetitions?

Draw around the word	If . . .	Choose one:
A circle	the word is a "to be" verb: is, am, are, was, were, be, being, been	Do not change. Change to a vivid verb. Do not change because the "to be" verb is in a quote or dialogue.
A rectangle	*the* begins a sentence	Do not change. Vary sentence beginning.

Sponge Activities

Sponge activities are quick three- to ten-minute activities that "soak up" time. They can be used during those last few minutes before the bell rings or when a team of students finishes before the others and they need to keep busy or practice a skill.

For example, a teacher may ask students to write a jingle, rap, poem, or flyer that reflects what they have learned about writing, giving the students seven minutes to prepare and write and three minutes to present.

Differentiated Growth Plan

Where does an EL start in the writing process in an all-English class? ELs should tackle the same writing assignments as all other students but on a much smaller scale at the beginning. For example, the ELs might write only one paragraph and use only three or four of the new vocabulary words and some invented spellings and creative grammatical structures for about the first three weeks of school. This will give the teacher time to analyze the students' writing and work out a plan of action with the students. The students can work on one or two skills per week, and the proofreading and editing will focus on these skills. Increasingly, the students and teacher will target other skills that can be assessed in the context of the whole-class assignment. Samples of skill mastery can be included in the students' portfolios. After a few months, the students' growth will be quite evident from the contents of the portfolios.

ELs should be part of the revising, editing, and proofreading processes as early as possible through modified roles. Although they cannot provide feedback at the beginning, ELs will learn by reading other students' work. Once they see other students actively participating in the proofreading and editing processes, they will want to take part as well. ELs will benefit from the peer input for revising their ideas, images, characters, and plot. If the revision stage proves to be a comfortable and productive endeavor, peer proofreading and editing will become a valuable vehicle for the new English writer.

Time will definitely be a factor in mastery of language and content. An EL cannot be expected to finish as many exercises as a fluent English speaker does. Exercises have to be carefully selected and trimmed down to a few good examples that reflect progress of skills and the content the student is working on.

ELs are handling three times as many variables and performing three times as many cognitive tasks in any one class as their peers. It is, therefore, critically important to help students feel free to experiment with language while they are learning content. The teacher's role is to make sure that there are ample opportunities for the ELs to practice through individual, paired, and cooperative activities.

Quick Tips for Teaching Writing

The sooner students begin writing, the faster they will make connections with the new language. However, the approach to writing must be carefully orchestrated. Make sure that ELs write after every subject area lesson.

During a student's initial writing phases in English, it is important to:

- Focus on the ideas the student has rather than those he or she lacks

- Provide opportunities for the student to interact with peers to question, analyze, speak up, and write down

- Set high but flexible standards

- Develop separate rubrics and criteria for this student's portfolio

Teachers can assist ELs in becoming good writers by:

- Making sure they comprehend the writing assignment, process, and outcomes

- Engaging students in a variety of prewriting activities that provide opportunities for ample discussion of new vocabulary, concepts, topics, or themes

- Responding often to what the students have written

- Allowing more time for ELs to develop, discuss, and share their writing with others

- Allowing joint authorships (pairs or small teams)

Reflection Questions

The following questions are provided to initiate discussions on the topics and processes mentioned in this chapter.

For Teachers

1. What types of writing strategies have been proven by research to be effective? Which are you using?

2. Make a list of adaptations or considerations for teaching writing to ELs. Discuss which are most appropriate for your students and grade level.

For Administrators

1. Does the school have an open policy for teaching writing, or is there one method that has to be used? Has that method been proven to be effective with ELs?

2. How can you support teachers as they experiment with new writing strategies that might be more appropriate for ELs and struggling writers?

For Universities and Departments of Education

1. What is the writing approach being promoted? How much research for ELs and struggling writers is behind it?

2. Are you sanctioning writing approaches out of habit or by evidence from your own action research?

CHAPTER NINE

Ensuring and Reinforcing Comprehension

Only about a third of America's eighth graders read at grade level, and 40 percent of those students who graduate from high school lack the literacy skills employers and universities seek (National Commission on Writing, 2005). For ELs, literacy becomes an even greater challenge if they have not acquired a solid education in the elementary grades. Given the overrepresentation of language-minority students among those struggling with literacy, it is important to identify those likely to have difficulty early to prevent them from falling behind (August & Shanahan, 2008).

Teachers ask students to read to acquire knowledge, yet, many times, reading becomes an end in itself. After students read a text, teachers need to follow up with strategies for anchoring knowledge to make sure that the students are learning the content they just read. In order to anchor knowledge, teachers must ensure comprehension through information-processing activities and strategies.

Teaching Techniques to Ensure Comprehension

Some of the best approaches used to teach and reach ELs focus on strategies that make the language comprehensible from the beginning, including hands-on activities, peer interaction, small-group learning, and technology. Such strategies enable students to hear, see, speak, and analyze new information in various ways and provide practice with the new learning. However, these activities alone are insufficient; the teacher plays a critical role in setting a safe context in which the students are willing to take risks with the new language and become actively engaged in learning all the time. The teacher's modeling and delivery of information or instruction can either be a hurdle or a clear path to student success (Calderón, 1992).

WHAT DOES THE RESEARCH SAY?

For ELs, oral language proficiency is important in the acquisition of skilled reading (August & Shanahan, 2008).

Proficiency includes both receptive and expressive skills and encompasses the use of phonology, vocabulary, morphology, grammar, and discourse features, as well as pragmatic skills (Lesaux, Kieffer, Faller, & Kelley, 2010).

Helping students build coherent representations of text ideas is a major focus of comprehension instruction (Beck, McKeown, & Kucan, 2005).

Strategy instruction that focuses on the memorization of strategies instead of on content learning does not help students (Murphy & Alexander, 2000).

Cognitive strategy instruction, along with meaningful text processing, helps students retain, organize, and evaluate the information that they read (RAND Reading Study Group, 2002; Palincsar & Brown, 1984).

When ELs engage in varying types of reading that reflect differing tasks, texts, and instructional objectives, their comprehension might be stifled because they do not understand the real goal for that reading task (Perfetti, Marron, & Foltz, 1996).

ELs need to know how to adjust goals when the concepts are new, when the task is long, or when the grammar is particularly complex (Grabe, 2009).

The teacher's delivery of instruction needs to be comprehensible regardless of the difficulty or complexity of the reading material or information being presented. Teachers can use any or all of the following sheltered-instruction techniques to help ELs make meaning, effectively interact, and internalize the new ways of developing oracy and functional discourse.

Teacher Speech

Comprehension is initiated through teacher talk. The way a teacher communicates with students facilitates or frustrates comprehension. The following strategies can be used to make instruction more comprehensible for ELs:

- Use a natural rate of speech but enunciate clearly. Be careful not to raise your volume.

- After presenting a process, sequence, or concept, repeat it with simpler and shorter sentences.

- Increase your use of rephrasing, repetition, clarification, restatement, and redundancy in the explanations or presentations of new material.

- While explaining, verbally emphasize new vocabulary, idioms, homo-phones, or abstract concepts, or write them on the board.

Contextualization in English

Abstract concepts are better understood when teachers use concrete examples that are already well known or can be easily understood. For example, teachers can provide visual reinforcement during an explanation through:

- Pantomime, gestures, and facial expressions

- Props and realia (real objects, such as a real "treasure box")

- SMART Board or whiteboard drawings, pictures, and online examples

- Photos and blackboard sketches

- Video clips and overhead transparencies

- Demonstrations and role-playing

- Hands-on, interactive tasks

- Graphic organizers on the board, such as story maps and word webs

Comprehension Checks

The teacher should verify comprehension of each instructional unit by checking for understanding frequently. Some techniques are:

- Asking "wh-" questions (who, what, where, when)

- Asking "proof" questions (How do you know that?)

- Asking "funny" questions (So, the head of the United States is called a king, right?)

- Confirming students' answers (Do you mean . . . ?)

- Asking for clarification or elaboration (Tell me more)

Directions in Dual-Language or Bilingual Classrooms

A teacher's speech in a dual-language or bilingual classroom is also critically important for accelerating the learning of academic language in two languages. While the use of code switching and Spanglish (a hybrid language combining words or idioms from Spanish and English) is a common bicultural norm of interaction (at home, in universities, in the business community), standard forms of Spanish and English should be the norm in schools. Keeping instruction in separate language blocks, either by days or weeks or subjects, helps students create a comfortable context for functioning in that language during that block and become truly bilingual, bicultural, and biliterate. Teachers may find the following list of reminders helpful:

- Give directions in English during the English block and in Spanish during the Spanish block. Do not translate; do not mix languages; do not preview or review in the other language.

- Break down complex tasks into simpler steps with specific instructions such as "Look at the story map. Point to the author box. Now point to the first event box. Let's read it together."

- Consistently model academic vocabulary and discourse for language arts, science, social studies, math, and other subject matters in both languages.

- Ask students to respond to your questions using words you have used or new words they read in their texts.

- Interrupt yourself frequently with questions to the students. This is a natural way to check for comprehension during an explanation or demonstration.

Student Interaction

We learn to speak a language through extensive verbal practice. Without ample student interaction time, teachers cannot ensure that a language is being learned. Therefore, it is important that teachers provide several opportunities for student interaction. Assign the students to pairs or groups and then ask them to summarize or clarify with their classmates or to teach each other. Ask for individual students to volunteer to restate what their classmates said. Other cooperative learning activities to generate different types of discourse can be found in chapter 10.

Error Correction

We all feel uneasy correcting or being corrected for errors. It is especially difficult for teachers of ELs because correcting their students might have detrimental outcomes; students might be too embarrassed to try again. Nevertheless, feedback is critical to improvement. Without feedback, there is no growth. The following guidelines can be used to prevent students from withdrawing or feeling embarrassed and thus refusing to try:

- Remind student peers that language errors are a necessary part of second-language acquisition.

- The teacher and student peers should concentrate on the message the students communicate, not the correctness of the message (function before form).

- If correction is absolutely necessary in the context of a class conversation, the restatement form (positive modeling technique) can be used. For instance, if the student says, "Does she has a pet?" then the teacher responds, "Does she have a pet? Yes, she does. She has a pet."

- Keep in mind that practice makes permanent. The more students practice pronouncing a word in a certain way, the more ingrained it becomes. Modeling pronunciation and helping students hear their pronunciation works along with practice.

Rich Language Development

If we want ELs to make adequate yearly progress, we must provide a rich language environment. This doesn't mean putting up word walls; it means providing different types of encounters with rich language and modeling rich conversations, for example:

- Conversations during which meaning is negotiated rather than simply transmitted

- Discussion instead of straight lecture or instructions

- Referential (open-ended) rather than display (closed-ended) questions; in the former, the teacher seeks new information ("What do you think this looks like?"), and in the latter, the teacher already knows the answer ("Where is the boy?")

- Personalized rather than impersonal conversation by using students' names when giving examples: "Let's say that Juan took a trip into the jungle," rather than, "We took a trip into the jungle."

Anchoring Reading and Vocabulary

Writing is one way to anchor the knowledge gained from reading and vocabulary. Small pieces of writing related to what students are reading can be introduced on a daily basis. The best strategy is to use an exit pass so you can quickly check what the students have written. Reading exit passes is easier than checking reading logs or journals. At the end of the lesson or before transitioning to a different subject, leave five to ten minutes for students to write a few lines on an exit pass.

An exit pass is usually one-quarter of a standard-size page. Assignments for exit passes can be as simple as: "Write two or three sentences about what you read and learned today" or "Write down five new sophisticated words you learned." For this, a simple blank exit pass (see fig. 9.1) suffices.

Name _____ Date _____

_____

_____

_____

Figure 9.1: Blank exit pass.

An exit pass can also include a combination of new words and the application of a comprehension strategy. Figure 9.2 is an example of an exit pass for cause and effect.

Assessment of Progress and Proficiency

The three types of assessments—entry-level, monitoring or formative, and summative—are tools to help teachers determine how well their students are progressing. Students' work should be carefully analyzed so that instruction can be geared toward ELs' level of language or reading stage. Teachers monitor students' progress so that the instructional program can be revised if students are not making adequate progress. To be most effective, curriculum, instruction, and assessment need to be coordinated.

Name _____ Date _____

It snowed more than two feet and caused many problems. The snow covered the cars, the streets, and the sidewalks. People could not drive their cars. People could not walk on the sidewalks. It was too slippery. The snow melted, causing floods and mudslides.

It snowed more than two feet and caused _____.

The snow covered _____.

People could not walk on the sidewalks because _____.

The snow melted and caused _____.

Figure 9.2: Exit pass for cause and effect.

At the beginning of the school year, entry-level assessments can inform teachers about the literacy and vocabulary levels of the students, can help teachers detect maturity and developmental needs of students, and can flag the strength of another language being used by the student or at home. Effective teachers ultimately use the results of entry-level assessments to plan instruction, select materials, and play with a variety of strategies to address the unique strengths that students bring to class.

Monitoring or formative assessments are checkpoints; their results point to what students have learned to date. Such assessments provide ongoing and timely measurements of students' progress and can quickly identify areas that need reteaching or extra support.

Summative assessments conducted at midyear or at the end of a school year are typically developed by experts outside of the classroom, such as text publishers or district evaluators. They are designed to assess how well students meet goals and standards, and assess big targets across multiple grade levels, schools, or districts.

Assessments are tools when they are used to inform and improve instruction. But they can also be harmful—when they are used to label children, when they are used inappropriately, or when they are seen as single measures of students' abilities. In too many cases, instruction is conducted in the primary language and the assessments are in English. This is inappropriate and unfair. In such cases, the results are not true indicators of either what the student knows or what the teacher has taught.

When assessing ELs, it is critical that the assessor understands what is being assessed and how. It is important to know if the results indicate a lack of knowledge of a specific skill that has been taught or a lack of understanding of the language and instructions for the test. For example, if the question is, "Explain how many ones are in the number ten," the student may know that the answer is ten but not have enough English vocabulary to "explain" his answer. So, he may not answer at all. A better phrasing may be, "Tell me how many ones are in the number ten." It is important that the assessor be fluent in the language and instruments being used to assess. On-the-spot or on-the-run translations when assessing a student should be avoided. If the translation is not prepared beforehand, improvised attempts often translate either the wrong concepts or the wrong level of difficulty. For example, a tester once translated "If you cut an apple in half, how many pieces do you get?" into "Si cortas una manzana en dos pedasos, cuantos pedasos tienes?" ("If you cut an apple in two pieces, how many pieces do you have?").

Assessment and evaluation are key components of the cycle of curriculum and instruction. They need to be part of the daily deliberations of all teachers. Textbooks, teacher guides, district documents, and state or provincial agency publications are great references for understanding how to develop or use the variety of assessments needed throughout the year.

Learning Targets

Assessing learning begins with the selection of "learning targets." The targets include the content, the language functions, and the cognitive strategies for reading and writing to be learned. Some questions to consider as you develop the assessments for learning targets:

- What do you want to hear and see the EL produce at the end of the week?

- How many words do you want the student to master verbally and to see in his or her writing?

- Write a list of words, cognitive skills, or content concepts you expect to be covered by the assessment. How will you assess prior knowledge?

- How will you assess the learning progress on these throughout the week?

- What opportunities for individual assessments can you build throughout your unit? For example, can you quickly assess one or two students while partner reading, at centers, or during independent reading?

There are a variety of activities and opportunities to assess even the most limited English proficient students for content learning: ask them to answer yes-no questions, ask them to point to correct responses, have a peer translate, ask the ESL specialist to help you assess the student, and so forth.

Assessing Vocabulary

Educators need to be quite strict and relentless when it comes to vocabulary. It is imperative that ELs show mastery of at least five words per subject per day; otherwise, their progress in learning English will be stunted. Word mastery means that the student:

- Can pronounce the word

- Can spell the word

- Knows the meaning and some of its multiple meanings or uses

- Recognizes it in the context of reading

- Know its usage in idioms or common phrases (upper grades)

- Uses it in classroom speech, discussions, and examples

- Uses it in written summaries or class writings without prompting or copying the word

Each week, routinely select five to ten words you have been teaching, and use the following steps to test the students' knowledge of the words:

1. Post the words and read each aloud.

2. Read each word and provide one to two minutes for students to define the word, give an example of it, use it in a sentence, or illustrate it.

3. Collect the students' papers.

4. Read each word and give its definition and an example.

5. Grade the papers and post the total class score. (Graphing the scores weekly gives students an extra math lesson and helps them become more interested and collegial.)

6. Reward the class as scores improve.

Assessing vocabulary is best accomplished in the context of usage. When students are discussing a topic, summarizing, or applying any of the functions of discourse, you can record words that the students use correctly. Select four students to listen to and record for a week, whenever they are interacting with peers. Select four others the following week. This will give you a good idea of the words students are mastering. The best test is to see which words are being included in their writing. If vocabulary words are not being used orally and in writing, the students probably haven't mastered them. If these words are important, they will need to be retaught.

Assessing Reading

Reading can be quickly and efficiently assessed during partner reading. As students practice their reading in pairs, alternating sentences and summarizing what they read at the end of each paragraph or page, the teacher can walk around and record their performance. The ExC-ELL program uses a protocol that contains categories such as fluency, use of new vocabulary words, use of different reading comprehension skills, and level of discourse. Teachers can use this or a similar protocol to easily document the real-time performance of two to four students each time students do partner reading. Then the observation protocols can be stored in each student's portfolio.

Assessing Writing

Students' basic development of narrative, informative, expository, and persuasive writing styles begin to develop early, and progress should be monitored. Teachers can assess students' writing in different ways. For example, table 9.1 is an example of a rubric that can be used to assess expository writing. Or, teachers can assess students' writing by level:

- Level 1—novice

- Level 2—intermediate

- Level 3—competent

- Level 4—exceptional

Each level can be defined according to the criteria of the assignment. Some students may be a level 4 in their native language and need to concentrate only on learning new words, such as transition words, idioms, and cultural referents, in English. Other students may be a level 1 in their own language. These students will need a lot of work with all aspects of literacy. They will need considerably more time and

Table 9.1: Rubric for Expository Writing

Conventions	Punctuation	Capitalization	Word Usage	Grammar/Syntax	Structure/Organization
Write legibly or create a document with no typos.	Put a period at the end of each telling sentence.	Capitalize proper nouns (names of people, pets, places, institutions, and so forth).	Use words that seem right when read aloud.	Use the correct verb form with each noun.	Select a purpose: Explain or inform / Persuade or argue a point/opinion
Make sure sentences are complete.	Put a question mark at the end of each question.	Capitalize the pronoun *I*.	Use synonyms instead of repeating words.	Use the correct word order in sentences (adjective, noun).	Select an organizational structure or format: Description / Sequence, chronological order / Cause and effect / Compare and contrast / Problem and solution
Begin sentences in different ways.	Put an exclamation mark at the end of exclamatory sentences.	Capitalize the first word in a sentence.	Use words that are precise/specific.	Use pronouns that agree with the gender of the noun.	Use a topic sentence to introduce the topic clearly.

more direct teaching to catch up with all others.

Writing can also be assessed on a daily basis with exit passes. The captured words, sentences, or paragraphs can be stored in the same way as the reading protocols. Every four weeks or so, the teacher can pull them out and do an analysis by simply noting the differences from one week to the next. If the differences are not significant and several students are exhibiting the same problems, that should trigger an instructional improvement strategy.

Respect for the Primary Language

In programs that use English as the primary language of instruction, it is critically important to show respect and status to the student's primary language and home culture. Language, culture, and identity are interwoven. Strategies that send the message that the student's primary language and culture are important and worthy of respect include:

- Encouraging the student to use his or her native language with language peers during activities to build comprehension but to be sure to use the new words in English once the task is understood

- Pairing a new student with a same-language buddy who is familiar with the classroom and school

- Using a variety of cooperative learning strategies to build acceptance of social norms and skills

- Motivating the student to teach his or her peers about his or her language and culture by sharing writings and projects

- Inviting the student's parents or other language peers as guest speakers

The more opportunities ELs have to share, read, and teach others their native language and culture, the greater their academic progress and self-esteem.

Reflection Questions

The following questions are provided to initiate discussions on the topics and processes mentioned in this chapter.

For Teachers

1. How do you ensure that students are learning language and subject-matter content?

2. What can you do to create a rich language environment?

3. Do you have a differentiated assessment process for the levels of EL proficiency?

4. How do you keep track of ELs' learning progress?

5. In bilingual settings, what is the policy and practice for using two or more languages?

For Administrators

1. Does your school promote ample student interaction and paired and team learning?

2. Do you have time during professional learning communities dedicated to analyzing EL writing?

3. Are your EL assessments aligned with language, literacy, and content standards?

4. In bilingual settings, have you established a policy for using two languages? Is that policy fully practiced? Does it need revision or reenergizing?

For Universities and Departments of Education

1. What should be added or revised in your writers' workshops and/or teacher preparation courses on writing development for ELs?

2. Are your faculty or specialists involved in redesigning assessments that would help schools improve practice by analyzing more relevant EL learning progressions?

3. Can you provide time and resources to schools so that teachers are better able to plan lessons together?

4. What philosophy and evidence-based practices do you promote for dual-language instruction? What messages are you giving the schools?

CHAPTER TEN

Cooperative Learning

By Liliana Minaya-Rowe

Educators struggle with the daily challenge of engaging those students who seem reluctant, disengaged, or apathetic in the classroom. These students appear to have a careless attitude about learning and succeeding at school. Sometimes they are labeled and excluded from participation in learning tasks. The underlying causes of students' reluctance are varied, complex, and often interrelated, particularly for upper elementary, middle, and high school students who are struggling with an array of socioemotional and interpersonal conflicts as they navigate the difficult period of adolescence. Elementary schools need to find the means to educate reluctant students, to address their needs, and to reach out to them before they get to middle school. This chapter highlights strategies to do just that.

Aligning With 21st Century Skills

To be effective educators of every child, whether motivated or apathetic, teachers must be equipped with strategies and develop behaviors that will enable the students. Teacher quality is essential in addressing student needs and reducing the achievement gap; research shows that teacher effectiveness is connected to overall educational quality and has a great impact on student achievement (Liston, Borko, & Whitcomb, 2008). For example, there is wide consensus that today's students need creativity and other 21st century skills in order to interact in a new age of technological advances, environmental awareness, and globalization (Pink, 2005; Rotherham & Willingham, 2009). A teacher who creates a cooperative learning environment that engages all students is likely to promote optimal learning for the 21st century.

The Partnership for 21st Century Skills (P21, www.p21.org), an organization that advocates for the teaching of 21st century skills, identified the knowledge and skills that students need to master in order to succeed in work and school of the

WHAT DOES THE RESEARCH SAY?

Some of the causes of lack of engagement in adolescent students are past negative experiences with education in elementary schools, negative feelings of self-efficacy that have been ingrained in their psyches, and their inability to form peer relationships (Guttman & Midgley, 2000; Nansel, Haynie, & Simons-Morton, 2003).

Teachers and school leaders can control these factors and influence the intrinsic and extrinsic motivation of students in positive ways by attempting to transform their disengagement (Brophy, 2004; Deci & Ryan, 2000).

Schools can help by undergoing profound change and development and controlling a positive school climate with elements such as teacher competency, task complexity, teacher-student relationships, and classroom complexity (Walsh, 2006).

Teachers' and administrators' attention to the unique needs of disengaged students can promote a school climate without violence or oppression (Farmer, 2003; Juvonen, 2007).

Schools can establish direct communication patterns in a cyclical fashion—for example, teachers respond to students who respond to teachers—to have an effect on the socialization of its members and to contribute to a positive school climate (Darling-Hammond, Meyerson, LaPointe, & Orr, 2010).

Schools today need to be accountable to the communities they serve, finding rigorous but effective methods of instruction while creating a climate of high expectation and meaningful learning (Chen & Weikart, 2008; National School Climate Council, 2007).

A number of age-related techniques and strategies exist to engage students in learning tasks. Classroom management, instructional strategies, and pacing the complexity are three components with complementary roles in teaching and learning; these components allow for students' learning challenges and engagement to be strategically differentiated to their specific individual needs (Marzano, 2007; Scherer, 2008).

Strategies and techniques that meet the linguistic and academic needs of ELs across levels of language proficiency are aligned with grade-level curriculum and content-area standards and built on the foundation of effective classroom management and full student participation (Calderón, 2007a).

future. The 21st century will require people to integrate basic skills with content knowledge as well as think independently, solve problems, and make decisions. P21 proposes essential skills and processes that will assist students in acquiring expertise in multidimensional abilities. The following are the four components of the framework described by P21 with suggestions of how cooperative learning can help students achieve in these areas:

1. **Core subjects and P21 century themes**. Cooperative learning strategies can be used frequently to organize and teach every type of content class, from math to reading to writing to science to global awareness to financial literacy.

2. **Learning and innovation skills**. Cooperative learning replaces individual seatwork, study, and drill. Students in cooperative groups work with each other and make sure that everyone in the group has mastered the concept. Cooperative learning is an excellent means for students to think critically, solve problems, create, and innovate.

3. **Information, media, and technology skills**. Cooperative learning strategies can be effective in classrooms with a wide range of performance levels in the present age of technology, media, and information. Heterogeneous groups work together to process information, build cognitive competencies, and engage in collaborative learning experiences to develop social skills. Teachers who leverage technology tools and incorporate cooperative learning strategies know how to guide students in ways to optimize learning and critical reasoning.

4. **Life and career skills**. Cooperative learning strategies benefit relationships between ELs and their peers. School satisfaction and optimal academic fulfillment are achieved through long-lasting gratifications that promote personal strengths, initiative, self-direction, and virtues.

Effective teachers use cooperative learning and classroom management strategies to promote the participation of every student in their classrooms.

Conditions for Productive Learning

Cooperative learning is a successful teaching and motivating strategy. Small teams composed of students with different levels of ability use a variety of learning activities to improve their understanding of a subject under low-anxiety conditions (Calderón, Hertz-Lazarowitz, & Slavin, 1998).

ELs at all levels of language proficiency can benefit from cooperative learning. Beginner ELs can use their first language as they build the academic and linguistic skills they need to make progress in the content area (Calderón, 1994; McGroarty & Calderón, 2005). Each team member is responsible for learning what is taught and for helping teammates learn. Cooperative learning is not an end in itself; it is a process that leads to learning (Slavin, 1995).

Teachers should set cooperative learning norms and protocols and remind students of what is expected of them during each activity (see table 10.1). Furthermore, teachers should set a focus on tasks, not roles. When students are given specific tasks, each is responsible for his or her own performance during the cooperative learning activity. The final product is the sum of individual performances to accomplish the concerted project (Calderón & Hertz-Lazarowitz, 1994; Sharan, 1994).

Table 10.1: Social Norms and Protocols in Cooperative Learning

Norms	Protocols
Everyone contributes ideas.	Respect others.
Everyone has a specific task (not a role).	Be positive.
Everyone learns from one another.	Accept opinions.
Everyone works with an open mind.	Contribute to the discussions.
	Help others.
	Accept help.
	Stay on task.
	Accept responsibility.

Role assignment is not productive in instruction as students are expected to perform in only one way during the activity. For example, "In this team, you are the writer; you are the discussant; you are the time keeper; you are the presenter." By dissecting the cooperative learning activity and assigning these roles, teachers limit the equal exposure, opportunity, and access to rigorous content all students need to have as well as their experience with reading, writing, discussing, and analyzing. The time keeper will only remind his or her peers how many minutes are left to complete the activity; he or she will not be directly involved with the academic work. The writer will have little or no opportunity to get involved in discussing, debating, and sharing opinions as he or she will have to focus on note taking only, and so on.

Cooperative learning is a needed resource in classrooms with ELs. Cooperative learning strategies can be used to engage ELs in motivating content-area settings while meeting important learning goals—as long as certain conditions for cooperative learning are met:

- **Positive interdependence**, or a "we are in this together" attitude; each team member's efforts are required and indispensable for team success, and each member contributes to the joint effort

- **Face-to-face interaction** to explain orally, teach one another, and check for understanding

- **Individual and group accountability** to prevent social loafing; each student makes an active contribution to the team

- **Interpersonal and small-group communication** for students to develop social skills for leadership, decision making, and trust building

- **Group processing** for a reflection on how well they are working together and how they might do better as a learning team (Johnson & Johnson, 1987)

Cooperative Learning in Content Classes

Cooperative learning strategies can be incorporated in math, science, social studies, and language arts classrooms to engage all students on vocabulary, reading, and writing development as part of a lesson, chapter, or unit. By using cooperative learning strategies in content classes, teachers can:

- Consolidate or anchor knowledge of the content lesson, so that all students know the content and use the correct terms and proper grammar

- Check whether everyone understood the content, what they know, what is still missing, and what needs to be done in future classes

- Assess and address the unique needs of their students, including those who are ELs and those who are reluctant to participate

The following selection of cooperative learning strategies can help strengthen a teacher's instruction. A teacher who employs these strategies enhances his or her effectiveness as interaction is provided through heterogeneous groupings.

A Medley of Cooperative Learning Strategies

There are many cooperative learning strategies and methods. Most language, literacy, and information-processing activities lend themselves to cooperative learning.

To ensure effectiveness, plan carefully and decide on the cooperative learning strategy ahead of time:

1. Select a cooperative learning strategy.

2. Identify the learning goals (grade-level contents and academic language).

3. Plan how to anchor knowledge and assess the students' level of understanding (individually and as a group).

4. Focus on knowledge and language skills to be taught (vocabulary, reading, writing, and grammar).

5. Decide how to group students.

6. Determine the materials needed and the time allocation.

Don't assume that students already know how to work in groups; show them how to work together. Be explicit about the value of cooperative learning; students need to know what benefits to expect from participating in this instructional strategy.

The research-based strategies in this section have proven successful in meeting the linguistic and academic needs of ELs across all levels of language proficiency (Calderón, 2007a). These strategies can be aligned with grade-level curriculum and content-area standards, and build on the foundation of effective classroom management. By using them in your lessons, you can balance nurturing with setting clear limits and high standards of responsibility in all your students. You can also encourage the students to be independent while guiding them without controlling. Consider adding these cooperative learning strategies to your repertoire.

Choose a cooperative learning activity that best fits your lesson and incorporate it in your plan. Before you begin the activity, remind your students of the social norms and protocols. Remind them of what is expected of them: "You have been assigned specific tasks. Each is responsible for his or her own performance, and each team member needs to contribute equally to the final product."

Eight Characteristics

The total time for this activity is 7 to 10 minutes. The instructions follow:

1. Students fold a piece of paper into eight rectangles.

2. Students write a characteristic about a specific aspect of the content in each of the rectangles (3 minutes).

3. Students move around and find a partner with matching characteristics (no talking) (2 minutes).

4. The partners walk together and find a set of partners who are different (2 minutes).

5. The two sets sit together as a team.

This activity and the next activity, the three-step interview, can be used at the beginning of the school year to form heterogeneous groupings. They can also be used during the year for reseating purposes or to start a new activity.

Three-Step Interview

The total time for this activity is 5 to 8 minutes. The instructions follow:

1. Students are in pairs. One acts as the interviewer and the other the interviewee (1 minute).

2. Students reverse roles (1 minute).

3. Students number off, one through four, and take turns sharing with the team what they learned about their partner in the interview (1 minute to introduce each).

Remind the interviewers to follow the interviewee's chosen topic, not to suggest others, and that the purpose of the interview is to gather information to share what each member of the team knows about the topic to his or her teammates. Instruct students and model how to look for themes in the interview responses that will help them capture the positive essence of the peer. Address the interview with a positive perspective: "Wonderful Ones, share what you have learned about Terrific Twos with your team. Thrilling Threes, share what you have learned about Fantastic Fours with your team."

Group Investigation

The total time for this activity is 30 to 120 minutes (over the course of a week). The instructions follow:

1. Students propose topics and categorize suggestions.

2. They organize into research groups to plan the learning task or subtopics for investigation.

3. Students gather and evaluate data and synthesize findings into a group report.

4. Each research group presents to the entire class and actively involves the audience.

5. Teachers and students evaluate student learning.

Group representatives form a steering committee to coordinate plans for the final report presentation. The teacher evaluates students' higher-level thinking about the subject they studied using criteria to gauge how students:

- Investigated aspects of the subject

- Applied their knowledge to the solutions of new problems

- Used inferences and questions requiring analysis and judgment

- Reached conclusions from sets of data

The teacher supports interpersonal dialogue and promotes an affective-social dimension of learning. His or her role during this activity is as a resource person and facilitator who models the social and communication skills expected from the students.

Random Numbers

The total time for this activity is 5 to 7 minutes. The instructions follow:

1. Students are divided into teams of four.

2. On a three-by-five-inch index card, students write their first name and three random numbers between one and twenty.

3. They share with their teams and make connections between the numbers they chose and their schoolwork. For example, if a student chose numbers

two, three, and five, he or she might say, "I am reading two short stories. Then I have to write a review with three paragraphs for each. Both reviews are due in five days." Or, if a student chose numbers twelve, four, and sixteen, he or she might say, "I used twelve of the sixteen new words, and four of them were cognates."

This activity can be used at the beginning of the class to build background knowledge and review concepts from previous classes.

In-House Jigsaw

The total time for this activity is 30 to 60 minutes. The instructions follow:

1. Students are divided into teams of four.

2. Each student is responsible for reading one part of a chapter or story or problem (10 minutes).

3. Each student maps key concepts and key words (10 minutes).

4. Each teaches the others in the team the information (3–5 minutes).

5. Each prepares one or two test questions (5 minutes).

Jigsaws can be used with any content that can be divided into sections. This jigsaw is a simple in-team activity; the teacher identifies a passage, text, or problem, and divides it into equal parts. Each team member becomes an expert on that part and reads, summarizes, and prepares to teach the team. Suggested activities include: reading a story, reading a chapter, writing a social studies narrative, writing a biography, and writing descriptive science or math material.

Expert Jigsaw

The total time for this activity is 30 to 60 minutes. The instructions follow:

1. Students count off at their tables and form expert teams (all the ones together, twos, threes, fours, and so on).

2. Each expert team is responsible for reading one part of a chapter or story or problem (5–10 minutes).

3. Each expert team studies, discusses, and summarizes the content (10 minutes).

4. Each prepares one or two test questions (5 minutes).

5. Each expert goes back to the home team and teaches the others (5 minutes each).

6. Each expert gives the test to the team (3 minutes).

7. The questions are used for the real test by the teacher.

By participating in this activity, students become motivated to study the material well and to work hard in their expert groups so that they can help their team do well. The key is interdependence. Every student depends on his or her teammates to provide the information needed to do well on the assessments.

Partners

The total time for this activity is 5 to 10 minutes. The instructions follow:

1. Students work in pairs to create or master content.

2. They consult with partners from other teams.

3. They then present their products or understandings with the other partner pair in their team.

When the teacher explains to the students that it is very important for them and their partners to do their best, they exert social pressure on one another to achieve. In this way, they maintain behavior that helps them succeed.

Line-Ups

The total time for this activity is 10 minutes. The instructions follow:

1. Students mill around and line up according to the task or question proposed by the teacher (for example, line up by birthdays; line up in alphabetical order; line up by the total sum of your math problems).

2. Students count off one to four, or as indicated, and form a team.

3. Teams sit together.

Tear-Ups

The total time for this activity is 20 to 40 minutes. The instructions follow:

1. Students are divided into teams of four.

2. Each team tears two sheets of different-colored construction paper into creative pieces.

3. Each student shares his or her piece with the team and talks about it. What does it look like?

4. Using all the pieces, teams write a group story with plot, characters, and setting.

5. Teams paste the pieces on another piece of construction paper or a large piece of chart paper, and write the story on the paste-up.

6. Teams share their stories.

This is a great writing activity. Students engage in a comprehensive writing project during which they work together as a team to plan, draft, revise, and edit their story. The writing activity helps ELs and reluctant students. They take part in mapping a story line, drawing a protagonist's personality, and adding visuals or drawings to the story. These visuals help them see the relationships they need to verbalize. You can also continue to motivate students when certain processes are just too difficult for them to write about by providing illustrations, guiding questions or prompts for vocabulary and use of grammar structures, prompt feedback to revise and edit, and guidance.

Corners

The total time for this activity is 5 to 10 minutes. The instructions follow:

1. Students count off one to nine. Ones go to one corner, twos to another, and so forth, to form triads.

2. Triads participate in timed team share (30 seconds each): the first student answers a question; the second student adds to the answer; the third student does the same (90 seconds). The process continues.

Corners is a quick activity that gets students out of their seats and gives them the opportunity to interact with other students. Pose selected questions to students with a set time so that they concentrate on the responses. Announce when it is time for the next person to answer or to add to what has already been said.

Tea Party

The total time for this activity is 10 to 15 minutes. The instructions follow:

1. Students count off one and two.

2. Ones form an inside circle, and twos form an outside circle. Each student

has a partner facing him or her.

3. Partners shake hands and discuss a question for one minute.

4. When the minute is up, partners say good-bye. One of the circles moves to the right. Each student has a new partner, and the process continues.

This activity is often used as a reward activity for student accomplishments. Teachers can bring in music and play it after the students say good-bye to the partner and before they say hello to the new partner. They can dance their way to meet the next partner.

Variations include:

- Concentric circles can be replaced by conga lines with the variation that a student at the head of the line dances his or her way to the end of the line if he or she so chooses while the peers clap to the tune.

- The inner circle is given the definition of the words, while the outer circle is given the vocabulary words. Partners work on the answer.

- When there is insufficient space, two or three concentric circles are formed in different areas of the class.

Classroom Management

As with cooperative learning, classroom management strategies support teaching and learning. As classroom managers, teachers set rules and procedures to encourage students to be orderly and respectful. Effective classroom management has been recognized as a crucial element in effective teaching.

In a well-managed classroom, teaching and learning can flourish. The teacher is responsible for creating such an atmosphere for students of all achievement levels. Here are some helpful tips:

- Recognize or reward successful teams. Your reward system could reward each student for improving his or her level of performance over his or her usual level. In this way, all students are motivated to do their best, and the system rewards improvement rather than ability so that every student can succeed based on his or her own efforts.

- Remember that each student is responsible for his or her own performance and development of content mastery, efficacy, and ownership in learning.

- Set up a scoring system that allows for students of all performance levels to contribute meaningfully to team scores or products.

- Team those students who present the least challenges in the classroom with those who need support. These two groups of students might otherwise be ignored in the classroom or be unwilling to learn because they might be perceived as unlikely to contribute much to the team score. This does not happen when an effective teacher structures activities to balance challenge and support to enhance the students' willingness to risk the hard work of real learning (Tomlinson, 2008).

Strategies for cooperative learning and classroom management go hand in hand. In cooperative learning groups, students are more academically productive, better behaved, and less likely to drop out (Center for Public Education, 2008). A caring classroom environment with high academic expectations is more effective in producing learning.

Reflection Questions

The following questions are provided to initiate discussions on the topics and processes mentioned in this chapter.

For Teachers

1. What classroom management strategies are working in your classroom? Do you need to try some new ones?

2. Which cooperative learning strategies help you manage your classroom in positive ways?

3. Do the cooperative learning strategies reach your ELs' language and academic needs? Are the ELs part of teamwork activities with native English speakers in your daily lessons?

For Administrators

1. In what ways can you support job-embedded professional development in your school so that classrooms have management plans aligned with cooperative learning and teaching that require 100 percent student involvement with the lesson?

2. What are the most important classroom management and cooperative learning strategies you need to see in your observations and walkthroughs?

3. How can you help your teachers see themselves as better teachers? What positive reward system should you implement?

For Universities and Departments of Education

1. How can you revise and update your teacher education programs to give high priority to classrooms with ELs and instill context-sensitive instructional practices that value and consider their needs and strengths?

2. Do your guidelines or core standards for EL instruction reflect a thorough approach in shared commitment by schools, universities, and families to educate ELs for 21st century challenges?

3. Do policies address equity and access for ELs to quality education with high academic learning? Do they respond to the continuous changes of student demographic trends?

REFERENCES AND RESOURCES

ACT. (2005). *Crisis at the core: Preparing all students for college and work.* Iowa City, IA: Author. Accessed at www.act.org/research/policymakers/pdf/crisis _report.pdf on January 14, 2011.

Aldridge, J. (2005). The importance of oral language. *Childhood Education, 81*(3), 177.

Asher, J. J. (1969). The total physical response approach to second language learning. *Modern Language Journal, 53*(1), 3–17.

Atwell, N. (1998). *In the middle: Writing, reading, and learning with adolescents* (2nd ed.). Portsmouth, NH: Heinemann.

Au, K. (2009/2010). Culturally responsive instruction. *Reading Today, 27*(3), 30–31.

August, D., Calderón, M., & Carlo, M. (2001). Transfer of reading skills from Spanish to English: A study of young learners. *National Association for Bilingual Education Journal, 24*(4), 11–42.

August, D., Goldenberg, C., & Rueda, R. (2010). Restrictive state language policies: Are they scientifically based? In P. Gándara & M. Hopkins (Eds.), *Forbidden language: English learners and restrictive language policies* (pp. 139–158). New York: Teachers College Press.

August, D., & Shanahan, T. (Eds.). (2006). *Developing literacy in second-language learners: Report of the National Literacy Panel on Language-Minority Children and Youth.* Mahwah, NJ: Lawrence Erlbaum.

August, D., & Shanahan, T. (Eds.). (2008). *Developing reading and writing in second-language learners: Lessons from the report of the National Literacy Panel on Language-Minority Children and Youth.* New York: Routledge.

Ballantyne, K. G., Sanderman, A. R., & McLaughlin, N. (2008). *Dual language learners in the early years: Getting ready to succeed in school.* Washington, DC: National Clearinghouse for English Language Acquisition. Accessed at www .ncela.gwu.edu/files/uploads/3/DLLs_in_the_Early_Years.pdf on November 23, 2010.

Barth, R. (1990). *Improving schools from within: Teachers, parents, and principals can make a difference.* San Francisco: Jossey-Bass.

Beck, I. L., & McKeown, M. G. (2001). Text talk: Capturing the benefits of read-aloud experiences for young children. *Reading Teacher, 55*(1), 10–20.

Beck, I. L., McKeown, M. G., & Kucan, L. (2002). *Bringing words to life.* New York: Guilford Press.

Beck, I. L., McKeown, M. G., & Kucan, L. (2005). Choosing words to teach. In E. H. Hiebert & M. L. Kamil (Eds.), *Teaching and learning vocabulary: Bringing research to practice* (pp. 207–222). Mahwah, NJ: Lawrence Erlbaum.

Beck, I. L., McKeown, M. G., & Omanson, R. C. (1987). The effects and uses of diverse vocabulary instructional techniques. In M. G. McKeown & M. E. Curtis (Eds.), *The nature of vocabulary acquisition* (pp. 147–163). Hillsdale, NJ: Lawrence Erlbaum.

Beck, I. L., Perfetti, C. A., & McKeown, M. G. (1982). The effects of long-term vocabulary instruction on lexical access and reading comprehension. *Journal of Educational Psychology, 74*(4), 506–521.

Benchmark Education Company. (2010). *Climate.* Pelham, NY: Author.

Bransford, J. D., Brown, A. L., & Cocking, R. R. (Eds.). (2001). *How people learn: Brain, mind, experience, and school.* Washington, DC: National Academies Press.

Brophy, J. (2004). *Motivating students to learn.* Mahwah, NJ: Lawrence Erlbaum Associates.

Calderón, M. (1984). *Training bilingual trainers: An ethnographic study of coaching and its impact on the transfer of training* [Doctoral dissertation]. Dissertation Abstracts and Claremont Graduate School / San Diego State University.

Calderón, M. (1992). *Sheltered instruction: Professional development manual for the State of Hawaii.* Honolulu, HI: Hawaiian State Department of Education.

Calderón, M. (1994). Mentoring, peer coaching, and support systems for first-year minority/bilingual teachers. In R. A. DeVillar, C. J. Faltis, & J. P. Cummins (Eds.), *Cultural diversity in schools: From rhetoric to practice* (pp. 117–141). Albany: University of New York Press.

Calderón, M. (1999). Teachers learning communities for cooperation in diverse settings. *Theory Into Practice, 38*(2), 94–99.

Calderón, M. (2007a). *Teaching reading to English language learners, grades 6–12: A framework for improving achievement in the content areas.* Thousand Oaks, CA: Corwin Press.

Calderón, M. E. (2007b). *RIGOR! Reading instructional goals for older readers: Reading program for 6th–12th students with interrupted formal education.* New York: Benchmark Education.

Calderón, M. (2009). Language, literacy and knowledge for ELLs. *Better: Evidence-Based Education, 1*(1), 14–15.

Calderón, M. E. (in press). Teaching writing to English language learners. In *Teaching writing to ELs in secondary schools.* Heslington, England: University of York.

Calderón, M., August, D., Slavin, R., Cheung, A., Duran, D., & Madden, N. (2005). Bringing words to life in classrooms with English language learners. In E. H. Hiebert & M. L. Kamil (Eds.), *Teaching and learning vocabulary: Bringing research to practice* (pp. 115–136). Mahwah, NJ: Lawrence Erlbaum.

Calderón, M., & Carreón, A. (1994). Educators and students use cooperative learning to become biliterate and bilingual. *Cooperative Learning, 14*(3), 6–9.

Calderón, M., & Carreón, A. (2001). A two-way bilingual program: Promise, practice, and precautions. In R. E. Slavin & M. Calderón (Eds.), *Effective programs for Latino children* (pp. 125–170). Mahwah, NJ: Lawrence Erlbaum.

Calderón, M. E., Carreón, A., Noyola, E., Cantú, J., Bishop, A., Minaya-Rowe, L., & Trejo, M. (2009). *Expediting Comprehension for English Language Learners (ExC-ELL): Manual for teachers.* Pelham, NY: Benchmark Education.

Calderón, M., Ford, M., Raphael, T., & Teale, W. (2010). *Wright Group LEAD21: Transforming K–5 literacy instruction for 21st century classrooms.* Chicago: Wright Group/McGraw-Hill.

Calderón, M., & Hertz-Lazarowitz, R. (1994). Implementing cooperative learning in the elementary schools: The facilitator's voice. In S. Sharan (Ed.), *Handbook of cooperative learning methods* (pp. 300–330). New York: Greenwood.

Calderón, M., Hertz-Lazarowitz, R., & Slavin, R. E. (1998). Effects of bilingual cooperative integrated reading and composition on students making the transition from Spanish to English reading. *Elementary School Journal, 99*(2), 153–165.

Calderón, M. E., & Minaya-Rowe, L. (2003). *Designing and implementing two-way bilingual programs: A step-by-step guide for administrators, teachers, and parents.* Thousand Oaks, CA: Corwin Press.

Calderón, M. E., & Minaya-Rowe, L. (2011). *Preventing long-term English language learners: Transforming schools to meet core standards.* Thousand Oaks, CA: Corwin Press.

Calderón, M. E., Sánchez, M., Quiroz, L. R., Jimenez, K., & Jennings, H. (2010a). *¡Imagínate!* Washington, DC: Office of English Language Acquisition.

Calderón, M. E., Sánchez, M., Quiroz, L. R., Jimenez, K., & Jennings, H. (2010b). *Anhelos y logros.* Washington, DC: Office of English Language Acquisition.

Calderón, M. E., Sánchez, M., Quiroz, L. R., Jimenez, K., & Jennings, H. (2010c). *Palabras/words.* Washington, DC: Office of English Language Acquisition.

Calderón, M., & Slavin, R. (2010, May). *Reading and language outcomes of a randomized evaluation of bilingual education programs: What do we mean by quality instruction?* Paper presented to the U.S. Department of Education, Washington, DC.

California Department of Education. (1999). *Reading/language arts frameworks for California public schools, kindergarten through grade twelve.* Sacramento: Author.

California Department of Education. (2000). *Mathematics frameworks for California public schools, kindergarten through grade twelve.* Sacramento: Author.

California Department of Education. (2003). *Science frameworks for California public schools, kindergarten through grade twelve.* Sacramento: Author.

California Department of Education. (2008). *Preschool learning foundations, volume 1.* Sacramento: Author.

California Department of Education. (2009). *Preschool English learners: Principles and practices to promote language, literacy, and learning—a resource guide.* Sacramento: Author.

California Department of Education. (2010). *California's common core content standards for English language arts and literacy in history/social studies, science, and technical subjects.* Sacramento: State Board of Education.

Carlo, M. S., August, D., & Snow, C. E. (2005). Sustained vocabulary-learning strategy instruction for English language learners. In E. H. Hiebert & M. L. Kamil (Eds.), *Teaching and learning vocabulary: Bringing research to practice* (pp. 137–154). Mahwah, NJ: Lawrence Erlbaum.

Center for Public Education. (2008). *Keeping kids in school: What research tells us about preventing dropouts.* Accessed at www.centerforpubliceducation.org/Main-Menu/Staffingstudents/Keeping-kids-in-school-At-a-glance/Keeping-kids-in-school-Preventing-dropouts.html on January 14, 2011.

Chall, J., & Dale, E. (1995). *Readability revisited.* Cambridge, MA: Brookline.

Chamberlin, M., & Plucker, J. (2008). P-16 education: Where are we going? Where have we been? *Phi Delta Kappan, 89*(7), 472–479.

Chen, G., & Weikart, L. A. (2008). Student background, school climate, school disorder, and student achievement: An empirical study of New York City's middle schools. *Journal of School Violence, 7*(4), 3–20.

Cunningham, A. E. (2005). Vocabulary growth through independent reading and reading aloud to children. In E. H. Hiebert & M. L. Kamil (Eds.), *Teaching and learning vocabulary: Bringing research to practice* (pp. 45–68). Mahwah, NJ: Lawrence Erlbaum.

Cunningham, A. E., & Stanovich, K. E. (1997). Early reading acquisition and its relation to reading experience and ability 10 years later. *Developmental Psychology, 33*(6), 934–945.

Darling-Hammond, L. (1997). *Doing what matters most: Investing in quality teaching.* Kutztown, PA: National Commission on Teaching and America's Future.

Darling-Hammond, L. (2000). Teacher quality and student achievement: A review of state policy evidence. *Education Policy Analysis Archives, 8*(1). Accessed at http://epaa.asu.edu/epaa/v8n1/ on October 4, 2010.

Darling-Hammond, L., Meyerson, D., LaPointe, M., & Orr, M. T. (2010). *Preparing principals for a changing world: Lessons from effective school leadership programs.* San Francisco: John Wiley & Sons.

Darling-Hammond, L., & Richardson, N. (2009). Teacher learning: What matters? *Educational Leadership, 66*(5), 46–53.

Deci, E., & Ryan, R. (2000). The "what" and "why" of goal pursuits: Human needs and the self-determination of behavior. *Psychological Inquiry, 11,* 227–268.

De La Paz, S., & Graham, S. (2002). Explicitly teaching strategies, skills, and knowledge: Writing instruction in middle school classrooms. *Journal of Educational Psychology, 94,* 291–304.

Dickinson, D., & Snow, C. (1995). *Teaching teachers about talk: The importance of conversation in preschool classrooms.* Boston: Education Development Center.

Duke, N. K., & Pearson, P. D. (2002). Effective practices for developing reading comprehension. In A. E. Farstrup & S. J. Samuels (Eds.), *What research has to say about reading instruction* (3rd ed., pp. 204–242). Newark, DE: International Reading Association.

Education Alliance. (1998). *Parental involvement: An overview of current literature.* Accessed at www.educationalliance.org/Research/ResearchParental Involvement.asp on January 14, 2011.

Ehri, L. C. (1994). Development of the ability to read words: Update. In R. B.

Ruddell, M. R. Ruddell, & H. Singer (Eds.), *Theoretical models and processes of reading* (4th ed., pp. 323–358). Newark, DE: International Reading Association.

Elmore, R. F. (2002). *Bridging the gap between standards and achievement.* New York: Albert Shanker Institute.

Epstein, J. L. (2005). A case study of the Partnership Schools Comprehensive School Reform (CSR) model. *Elementary School Journal, 106*(2), 151–170.

Family Literacy Support Network. (2009). *Telling our stories: Program practices come to life.* Downey, CA: Los Angeles County Office of Education.

Farmer, P. (2003). *Pathologies of power: Health, human rights, and the new war on the poor.* Berkeley: University of California Press.

Florida Center for Reading Research. (2005). *Differentiated reading instruction: Small group alternative lesson structures for All students.* Tallahassee, FL: Author. Accessed at www.fcrr.org/assessment/pdfsmallgroupalternativelesson structures.pdf on January 14, 2011.

Francis, D. J., Rivera, M. O., Moughamian, A. C., & Lesaux, N. K. (2008). *Effective interventions for reaching reading to English language learners and English language learners with disabilities: Guidance document.* Portsmouth, NH: RMC Research Corporation, Center on Instruction.

Fuchs, L. S., & Fuchs, D. (1993). Formative evaluation of academic progress: How much growth can we expect? *School Psychology Review, 22*(1), 27–48.

Garcia, G. E., & Godina, H. (2004). Addressing the literacy needs of adolescent English language learners. In T. Jetton & J. Dole (Eds.), *Research and practice in adolescent literacy* (pp. 304–320). New York: Guilford Press.

Genesee, F., Lindholm-Leary, K., Saunders, W., & Christian, D. (2005). English language learners in U.S. schools: An overview of research findings. *Journal of Education for Students Placed at Risk, 10*(4), 363–385.

Gormley, W. T., Phillips, D., & Gayer, T. (2008). Preschool programs can boost school readiness. *Science, 320*(5884), 1723–1724.

Gottlieb, M., Cranley, M. E., & Cammilleri, A. (2007). *Understanding the WIDA English Language Proficiency Standards: A resource guide—PreKindergarten through grade 12.* Madison, WI: Board of Regents of the University of Wisconsin System. Accessed at www.wida.us/standards/Resource_Guide _web.pdf on January 14, 2011.

Grabe, W. (2009). *Reading in a second language: Moving from theory to practice.* Cambridge, England: Cambridge University Press.

Graham, S., & Hebert, M. (2010). *Writing to read: Evidence for how writing can improve reading— A report from Carnegie Corporation of New York.* Washington, DC: Alliance for Excellent Education.

Graham, S., & Perin, D. (2007). *Writing next: Effective strategies to improve writing of adolescents in middle and high schools.* New York: Carnegie Corporation of New York. Accessed at www.aiceonline.com/Resources/Writing-Grade%20 4–12.pdf on November 16, 2010.

Graves, M. F. (1986). Vocabulary learning and instruction. *Review of Research in Education, 13,* 49–89.

Graves, M. F. (2006). *The vocabulary book: Learning and instruction.* New York: Teachers College Press.

Guttman, L. M., & Midgley, C. (2000). The role of protective factors in supporting the academic achievement of poor African American students during the middle school transition. *Journal of Youth and Adolescence, 29*(2), 223–248.

Hamre, B. K., Pianta, R. C., Mashburn, A. J., & Downer, J. T. (2007). *Building a science of classrooms: Application of the CLASS Framework in over 4,000 U.S. early childhood and elementary classrooms.* Charlottesville, VA: University of Virginia. Accessed at www.icpsr.umich.edu/files/PREK3RD/resources/pdf /BuildingAScienceOfClassroomsPiantaHamre.pdf on October 4, 2010.

Harris, K., & Graham, S. (1996). *Making the writing process work: Strategies for composition and self-regulation* (2nd ed.). Cambridge, MA: Brookline.

Hart, B., & Risley, T. (1995). *Meaningful differences in the everyday lives of young American children.* Baltimore: Brookes.

Harvard Family Research Project. (2006). *Family involvement in early childhood education.* Accessed at www.hfrp.org/publications-resources/browse-our -publications/family-involvement-in-early-childhood-education on January 14, 2011.

Hiebert, E. H., & Kamil, M. L. (Eds.). (2005). *Teaching and learning vocabulary: Bringing research to practice.* Mahwah, NJ: Lawrence Erlbaum.

Hill, H. C., Rowan, B., & Ball, D. L. (2005). Effects of teachers' mathematical knowledge for teaching on student achievement. *American Educational Research Journal, 42*(2), 371–406.

Hoover-Dempsey, K., & Sandler, H. (1997). Why do parents become involved in their children's education? *Review of Educational Research, 67*(1), 3–42.

Horowitz, S. H. (2008). *An updated library of helpful resources.* Accessed at www .ncld.org/ld-basics/ld-explained/basic-facts/an-updated-library-of-helpful -resources on October 4, 2010.

Johnson, D. W., & Johnson, R. T. (1987). *Cooperation and competition: Theory and research.* Edina, MN: Interaction Book Company.

Joyce, B., & Showers, B. (2002). *Student achievement through staff development* (3rd ed.). Alexandria, VA: Association for Supervision and Curriculum Development.

Juvonen, J. (2007). Reforming middle schools: Focus on continuity, social connectedness, and engagement. *Educational Psychologist, 42*(4), 197–208.

Lara-Alecio, R., Irby, B. J., & Tong, F. (2010, May). *Project ELLA: The results of a five-year randomized trial study.* Presented at the annual meeting of the American Educational Research Association, Denver, CO.

Lesaux, N. K., Kieffer, M. J., Faller, S. E., & Kelley, J. G. (2010). The effectiveness and ease of implementation of an academic vocabulary intervention for linguistically diverse students in urban middle schools. *Reading Research Quarterly, 45*(2), 196–228.

Liston, D., Borko, H., & Whitcomb, J. (2008). The teacher educator's role in enhancing teacher quality. *Journal of Teacher Education, 59*(2), 111–116.

Marzano, R. J. (2007). *The art and science of teaching: A comprehensive framework for effective instruction.* Alexandria, VA: Association for Supervision and Curriculum Development.

Mashburn, A., Hamre, B., Pianta, R., & Downer, J. (2007, March). *Building a science of classrooms: Three dimensions of child-teacher interactions in PK–3rd grade classrooms.* Paper presented at the biennial meeting of the Society for Research in Child Development, Boston, MA.

McGroarty, M., & Calderón, M. (2005). Cooperative learning for second language learners. In P. A. Richard-Amato & M. A. Snow (Eds.), *Academic success for English language learners* (pp. 174–194). Upper Saddle River, NJ: Pearson Education.

Murphy, P., & Alexander, P. (2000). A motivated exploration of motivation terminology. *Contemporary Educational Psychology, 25,* 3–53.

Nagy, W. (2005). Why vocabulary instruction needs to be long-term and comprehensive. In E. H. Hiebert & M. L. Kamil (Eds.), *Teaching and learning vocabulary: Bringing research to practice* (pp. 27–44). Mahwah, NJ: Lawrence Erlbaum.

Nagy, W. E., & Herman, P. A. (1987). Breadth and depth of vocabulary knowledge: Implications for acquisition and instruction. In M. G. McKeown & M. E. Curtis (Eds.), *The nature of vocabulary acquisition* (pp. 19–35). Hillsdale, NJ: Lawrence Erlbaum.

Nansel, T., Haynie, D., & Simons-Morton, B. (2003). The association of bullying and victimization with middle school adjustment. *Journal of Applied School Psychology, 19*(2), 45–61.

National Clearinghouse for English Language Acquisition. (2008). *The growing numbers of English learner students.* Washington, DC: Author. Accessed at www.ncela.gwu.edu/files/uploads/9/growingLEP_0708.pdf on October 4, 2010.

National Commission on Writing. (2005). *Writing: A powerful message from state government.* New York: College Board. Accessed at www.collegeboard.com /prod_downloads/writingcom/powerful-message-from-state.pdf on January 14, 2011.

National Commission on Writing. (2006). *Writing and school reform.* New York: College Board. Accessed at www.collegeboard.com/prod_downloads/writing com/writing-school-reform-natl-comm-writing.pdf on January 14, 2011.

National Governors Association Center for Best Practices & Council of Chief State School Officers. (2010). *K–12 Common Core State Standards.* Accessed at www.corestandards.org on January 14, 2011.

National Institute for Literacy. (2009). *Learning to talk and listen: An oral language resource for early childhood caregivers.* Washington, DC: Author.

National Reading Panel. (2000). *Teaching children to read: An evidence-based assessment of the scientific research literature on reading and its implications for reading instruction* (National Institutes of Health Publication No. 00–4769). Washington, DC: National Institute of Child Health and Human Development.

National Research Center on Learning Disabilities. (2007). *Core concepts of RTI.* Accessed at www.nrcld.org/about/research/rti/concepts.html on October 20, 2010.

National Research Council. (2010). *Preparing teachers: Building evidence for sound policy.* Washington, DC: National Academies Press.

National School Climate Council. (2007). *The school climate challenge: Narrowing the gap between school climate research and school climate policy, practice guidelines and teacher education policy.* New York: Author. Accessed at www .ecs.org/html/projectsPartners/nclc/docs/school-climate-challenge-web.pdf on January 14, 2011.

Ortiz, A. A., & Artiles, A. J. (2010). Meeting the needs of ELLs with disabilities: A linguistically and culturally responsive model. In G. Li & P. A. Edwards (Eds.), *Best practices in ELL instruction* (pp. 247–272). New York: Guilford Press.

Palincsar, A., & Brown, A. (1984). Reciprocal teaching of comprehension-fostering and comprehension-monitoring activities. *Cognition and Instruction, 1,* 117–175.

Pearson, P. D., & Fielding, L. (1991). Comprehension instruction in the primary grades. In C. Block & M. Pressley (Eds.), *Comprehension instruction: Research-based practices* (pp. 247–258). New York: Guilford Press.

Peregoy, S. F., & Boyle, O. F. (2008). *Reading, writing, and learning in ESL: A resource book for K–12 teachers.* Boston: Allyn & Bacon.

Perfetti, C., Marron, M., & Foltz, P. (1996). Sources of comprehension failure: Theoretical perspectives and case studies. In C. Cornoldi and J. Oakhill (Eds.), *Reading comprehension difficulties* (pp. 137–165). Mahwah, NJ: Lawrence Erlbaum.

Persky, H. R., Daane, M. C., & Jin, Y. (2003). *The nation's report card: Writing 2002* (NCES 2003–529). Washington, DC: U.S. Department of Education, Institute of Education Sciences, National Center for Education Statistics.

Pianta, R. C., & Hamre, B. K. (2009). Classroom processes and positive youth development: Conceptualizing, measuring, and improving the capacity of interactions between teachers and students. *New Directions for Youth Development, 2009*(121), 33–46.

Pink, D. (2005). *A whole new mind.* New York: Riverhead Books.

Pressley, M. (1997). The cognitive science of reading. *Contemporary Educational Psychology, 22,* 247–259.

RAND Reading Study Group. (2002). *Reading for understanding: Toward an R&D program in reading comprehension.* Accessed at www.rand.org/pubs /monograph_reports/MR1465.html on January 14, 2011.

Rasinski, T. (2011, May). *Whatever happened to the art of teaching reading?* Presented at the annual meeting of the International Reading Association, Orlando, FL.

Raudenbush, S. (2009). The Brown legacy and the O'Connor challenge: Transforming schools in the images of children's potential. *Educational Researcher, 38*(3), 169–180.

Robbins, C., & Ehri, L. (1994). Reading storybooks to kindergartners helps them learn new vocabulary words. *Journal of Educational Psychology, 86,* 54–64.

Rotherham, A. J., & Willingham, D. (2009). 21st century skills: The challenges ahead. *Educational Leadership, 67*(1), 16–21.

Rydland, V., & Aukrust, V. G. (2005). Lexical repetition in second language learners' peer play interaction. *Language Learning, 55*(2), 229–274.

Samuels, S. J. (1979). The method of repeated readings. *The Reading Teacher, 32,* 403–408.

Saunders, W., & Goldenberg, C. (2010). Research to guide English language development instruction. In *Improving education for English learners: Research-based approaches.* Sacramento: California Department of Education.

Scherer, M. (2008). Ode to positive teachers. *Educational Leadership, 66*(1), 7.

Sénéchal, M., & Cornell, E. H. (1993). Vocabulary acquisition through shared reading experiences. *Reading Research Quarterly, 28,* 360–374.

Sharan, S. (1994). *Group investigation: Expanding cooperative learning.* New York: Teachers College Press.

Shore, R. (2009). *PreK–3rd: Teacher quality matters* (Policy to Action Brief No. 3). New York: Foundation for Child Development.

Slavin, R. E. (1995). *Cooperative learning: Theory, research and practice* (2nd ed.). Boston: Allyn & Bacon.

Slavin, R. E., & Cheung, A. (2005). A synthesis of research on language of reading instruction for English language learners. *Review of Educational Research, 75*(2), 247–284.

Slavin, R. E., & Madden, N. A. (2001). *One million children: Success for all.* Thousand Oaks, CA: Corwin Press.

Slavin, R. E., Madden, N., Calderón, M., Chamberlain, A., & Hennessy, M. (2010, April). *Reading and language outcomes of a five-year randomized evaluation of transitional bilingual education?* Paper presented at the conference of the American Educational Research Association, Denver, CO.

Society for Neuroscience. (2008, September). The bilingual brain. *Brain Briefings.* Washington, DC: Author.

Sohn, E. (2004). A change in climate. *Science News for Kids.* Accessed at www .sciencenewsforkids.org/articles/20041208/Feature1.asp on January 18, 2011.

Stahl, S. A., & Fairbanks, M. M. (1986). The effects of vocabulary instruction: A model-based meta-analysis. *Review of Educational Research, 56*(1), 72–110.

Stahl, S. A., & Nagy, W. (2006). *Teaching word meanings.* Mahwah, NJ: Lawrence Erlbaum.

Stanovich, K. E. (1994). Constructivism in reading education. *Journal of Special Education, 28*(3), 259–274.

Stenberg, R. J. (1987). Most vocabulary is learned from context. In M. G. McKeown & M. E. Curtis (Eds.), *The nature of vocabulary acquisition* (pp. 89–105). Hillsdale, NJ: Erlbaum.

Tabors, P. O. (2008). *One child, two languages: A guide for childhood educators of children learning English as a second language* (2nd ed.). Baltimore: Brookes.

Tabors, P. O., & Snow, C. E. (2001). Young bilingual children and early literacy development. In S. B. Neuman & D. K. Dickinson (Eds.), *Handbook of early literacy research* (pp. 159–178). New York: Guilford Press.

Takanishi, R., & Kauerz, K. (2008). PK inclusion: Getting serious about a P–16 education system. *Phi Delta Kappan, 89*(7), 480–487.

Tomlinson, C. A. (2008). The goals of differentiation. *Educational Leadership, 66*(3), 26–30.

Vaughn, S. (n.d.). *Response to intervention in reading for English language learners.* Accessed at www.rtinetwork.org/learn/diversity/englishlanguagelearners on November 23, 2010.

Walsh, F. (2006). A middle school dilemma: Dealing with "I don't care." *American Secondary Education, 35*(1), 5–15.

Zwiers, J. (2008). *Building academic language: Essential practices for content classrooms.* San Francisco: Jossey-Bass.

INDEX

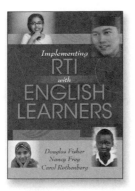

Implementing RTI With English Learners
Douglas Fisher, Nancy Frey, and Carol Rothenberg

Learn why RTI is the ideal framework for supporting English learners. Follow the application and effectiveness of RTI through classroom examples and the stories of four representative students of varying ages, nationalities, and language proficiency levels.
BKF397

Making Math Accessible to English Language Learners
r4 Educated Solutions

Help English language learners build academic vocabulary and proficiency in meaningful mathematics while keeping the entire class engaged. A great tool for strengthening classroom instruction, this manual offers research-based strategies that address the affective, linguistic, and cognitive needs of ELLs.
K–2 BKF284, 3–5 BKF285, 6–8 BKF286, 9–12 BKF287

40 Reading Intervention Strategies for K–6 Students
Elaine K. McEwan-Adkins

This well-rounded collection of reading intervention strategies, teacher-friendly lesson plans, and adaptable miniroutines will support and inform your RTI efforts. Many of the strategies motivate all students as well as scaffold struggling readers. Increase effectiveness by using the interventions across grade-level teams or schoolwide.
BKF270

Rebuilding the Foundation
Edited by Timothy V. Rasinski

Teaching reading is a complex task without a simple formula for developing quality instruction. This book presents a deep and thoughtful conversation about what is meant by effective reading instruction for all students. Rather than build on or alter existing models, this book considers how educators and policymakers might think about rebuilding and reconceptualizing reading education, perhaps from the ground up.
BKF399

Wait! Your professional development journey doesn't have to end with the last pages of this book.

We realize improving student learning doesn't happen overnight. And your school or district shouldn't be left to puzzle out all the details of this process alone.

No matter where you are on the journey, we're committed to helping you get to the next stage.

Take advantage of everything from **custom workshops** to **keynote presentations** and **interactive web and video conferencing**. We can even help you develop an action plan tailored to fit your specific needs.

Let's get the conversation started.

Call 888.763.9045 today.

 solution-tree.com